Young England: The New Generation

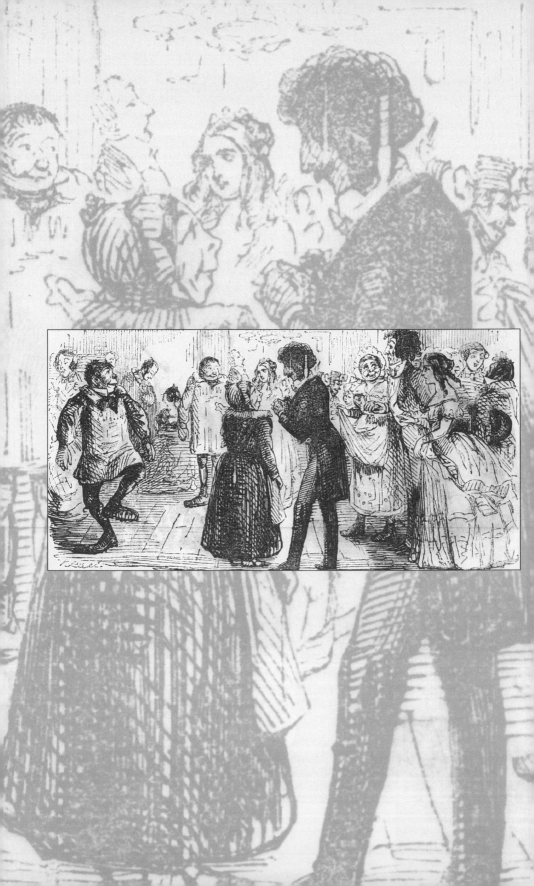

Young England

The New Generation

A Selection of Primary Texts

Edited by

John Morrow

Leicester University Press
London and New York

*For my sister Mary, and
my brothers, Andrew, Jim and Peter*

First published 1999 by

Leicester University Press, *A Cassell imprint*
Wellington House, 125 Strand, London WC2R 0BB
370 Lexington Avenue, New York, NY 10017–6550

© Introduction and editorial apparatus John Morrow 1999
© Contributions as per copyright holders

British Library Cataloguing in Publication Data

A catalogue record for this book is available from the British Library.

ISBN   0 7185 0145 4 (hardback)
ISBN   0 7185 0146 2 (paperback)

Library of Congress Cataloging-in-Publication Data

Young England: the new generation: a selection of primary texts /
    edited by John Morrow.
        p.   cm.
      Includes bibliographical references and index.
      ISBN   0–7185–0145–4 (hardcover).—ISBN   0–7185–0146–2 (paperback)
      1.   Great Britain—Politics and government—1837–1901—Sources.
    2.   Conservatism—Great Britain—History—19th century—Sources.
    3.   Conservative Party (Great Britain)—History—Sources.   4. Young England
    movement—Sources.   I.   Morrow, John, Ph. D.
    DA559.7.Y68   1999
    941.081—dc21   98–53992
                                                                                    CIP

TITLE PAGE: 'Young England Soirée'. (*From the Alexander Turnbull Library, National
Library of New Zealand, Te Puna Mātauranga o Aotearoa, ref no. S-L 189.) Punch*
predicted that Young England's penchant for the integration of classes at social and
recreational events would be one of the 'bubbles' of 1845.

Designed and typeset by Ben Cracknell Studios
Printed and bound in Great Britain by
Biddles Ltd, Guildford and King's Lynn

Contents

List of Illustrations

Preface

This volume provides readers with access to a range of primary material produced by parliamentary and extra-parliamentary members of 'Young England'. Extracts from the writings and speeches of Young England figures are supplemented by reviews and commentaries illustrating contemporary responses to the movement. The texts printed here are drawn from diverse sources, some are very rare, and many of which are available only in a few specialized research libraries. It is hoped that this collection will provide a useful resource for scholars and students interested in early Victorian political and intellectual history.

Young England ideas were conveyed in poetry, speeches, occasional pieces and pamphlets, rather than in systematic treatises, and so the writings of members of the group are invariably marked by repetitions and *longueurs*. In order to take account of this, and to make the best use of the space available, the more important texts printed here have been abridged considerably, and other material has been edited into extracts, some of which are very brief. These economies have made it possible to include a comprehensive range of material without, it is hoped, giving a distorted picture of the aspirations and views of the 'New Generation'.

Since Benjamin Disraeli's Young England trilogy is available in modern editions, selections drawn from it play only a very minor role in this book. Of the other members of the movement, Lord John Manners and George Smythe were most important and most prolific. Consequently, the prose, and to a lesser extent the poetry, of Manners and Smythe have a prominent place in this collection. However, their writings and speeches are supplemented by those of Alexander Baillie Cochrane, William Busfield Ferrand, Richard Monckton Milnes and unknown figures belonging to extra-parliamentary

Young England. The texts are organized in four themes, each of which is divided into sub-themes that focus on distinctive aspects of the Young England programme and responses to it.

In the process of collecting and editing this material and writing the Introduction to the volume, I have incurred a number of debts that I am pleased to have this opportunity to acknowledge. Work on this project has been assisted materially by research grants and grants in aid of travel provided by the Internal Grants Committee of Victoria University, by the Research Committee of the Faculty of Humanities and Social Sciences, and from funds controlled by the Vice Chancellor of the University. I am very grateful for this support. The staff of Victoria University Library, and particularly Justin Cargill, Guy Reynolds and Anne Squires of its Reference Department, have provided their customarily high level of courteous and professional service. I have also gained invaluable assistance from staff of the Alexander Turnbull Library and the Parliamentary Libraries in Wellington, and the Bodleian, British, British Newspaper, and Cambridge University Libraries in England. I must thank the Trustees of the National Trust for permission to quote from the Disraeli papers, and the Alexander Turnbull Library for allowing me to obtain illustrations from materials in its collections.

Anne and Jonathan Scott very kindly took time from their own work to hunt out some material for me in the Cambridge Library. They also extended their generous hospitality to me when I undertook research there. I am very grateful to Myre Ruben for arranging accommodation for me in Oxford. As in the past, my parents and other members of my family, and Peter and Issie Mahoney, entertained me at various times during my research leave. Jonathan Boston, Susan Grogan, Philip Knight, Jean-Marc Lecaudé, Pat Maloney (all of Victoria University), Marie Peters of the University of Canterbury, and Miles Taylor of King's College, London, responded promptly and helpfully to queries. Adrienne Nolan and Theresa Rogers provided cheerful and effective secretarial assistance. Jonathan Scott and Mark Francis offered valuable comments on a draft of the Introduction and my wife Di has grappled with a number of different versions of this essay. As usual, she has given me the benefit of her scholarly judgement and the comfort of her support. These people have saved me from a whole host of errors and infelicities of style, but responsibility for the remaining imperfections of this volume lies with the editor.

John Morrow
Wellington, New Zealand
March 1998

A Note on the Texts

The texts produced here are all extracted from the originals. The sources from which this material is drawn are indicated in short form in endnotes; full references are in the Bibliography. Citations from manuscript sources and parliamentary debates, source references, identifications of individuals mentioned in the texts and elucidation of contextual details and historical references are placed in endnotes. All other references and cross-references appear in short form in parenthesis in the text. In order to facilitate alignment of the texts with the sources from which they are drawn, the pagination of the latter is indicated by in-text bold numerals set in square brackets.

Introduction

I *The Young England Project*

Between 1842 and 1845 Sir Robert Peel's government was subject to critical scrutiny by four backbench MPs known as the 'Young England Party'. This group never saw itself as a parliamentary faction and was armed with an ambitious agenda: it wished to generate a reinvigorated national political and social culture that would offer fresh hope for the future. Despite its Tory attachments, Young England defined itself by evoking a counter-image of 'Old England' that was neither benign nor bucolic. For members of the 'new generation' the last century and a half of English history had been disfigured by the emergence of a corrupt pseudo-aristocratic oligarchy that detached itself from the rest of the community and reduced a succession of monarchs to the status of tawdry ciphers. This oligarchy was spawned by the misnamed Glorious Revolution of 1688 and its rise coincided with the financial revolution of the 1690s. Later it nurtured attitudes towards wealth and social responsibility that made late-eighteenth-century advances in productive techniques a bane rather than a blessing for large sections of the community.

Although aspects of Young England's critique echoed Country Party themes, the movement was very far from being merely a throwback to the opposition politics of the previous century.[1] Like revivalist figures in French and German political romanticism, the 'new generation' in England sought to recreate the idea of a national community by tempering rationalistic tendencies (associated with Calvinism and the Enlightenment) with human sympathies that sprang from the imagination. They were also suspicious of the eighteenth-century alliance between church and state, and wished to refurbish the images of monarchy, aristocracy and the national church so that they could form the basis of a social and political order that was generally beneficial. Since this order would be conducive to human happiness, Christian responsibility and social harmony, it provided a framework in which progressive tendencies could be related positively to the interests of the whole community.

The original, and on some accounts the only true members of Young England were Benjamin Disraeli, then a well-known novelist with considerable parliamentary experience, the Honourable George Smythe, Lord John Manners and Alexander Baillie Cochrane. All these men were youthful and recently elected MPs, and all had literary as well as political interests. Disraeli laid claim to an aristocratic ancestry from a Venetian enclave of the Jewish Diaspora, while the other members of the party had more conventional and less fanciful origins in the English, Irish and Scottish nobility.[2] In their parliamentary endeavours Disraeli and his colleagues were supported by varying numbers of other Conservative MPs. Four of these men, Alexander Beresford-Hope, William Busfield Ferrand, Peter Borthwick and Richard Monckton Milnes, were most often identified with the party and, in a loose sense at least, can be said to have been members of it.[3] The Young England group in the House of Commons was supported by John Walter of *The Times* and had a close relationship with the proprietor of the *Morning Post* (Lamington 1906, pp. 202, 154, 158).

Although Young England rose to prominence as a parliamentary movement, it also acquired a presence away from Westminster. Sometimes (as in Bingley in Ferrand's native Yorkshire) extra-parliamentary Young Englandism was fostered directly by parliamentary figures (see Ward 1965–6). In other cases, however, it was a consequence of independent initiatives. For example, the short-lived weekly *Young England, or, The Social Condition of the Empire* focused on the social aspects of the Young England programme, developing independent lines on capital punishment and on the unfair abuse suffered by the medical profession. More significantly, it was occasionally sceptical of the nostalgic yearnings and aristocratic understanding of hierarchy that loomed so large in the public statements of Lord John Manners and his friends (see below, p. 126).[4] The promoters of this publication showed signs of wishing to transform Young England into a national mass movement, but members of the parliamentary party did not encourage this aspiration.[5] Disraeli, Cochrane, Manners and Smythe did not think that their wish to change the political attitudes of their contemporaries, and to purify and revitalize the nation's political culture, would lead to experiments in political organization.

During 1845 the parliamentary party began to lose its shape and was broken irretrievably in early 1846 by the crises over the repeal of the Corn Laws. The post-repeal split between the Peelites and the rest of the Conservative Party meant that Young England could no longer play a mediating and invigorating role in Parliament, while the defection of some leading Tractarians to the Roman Catholic Church made its aspirations to reform Anglicanism seem increasingly unrealistic. There were also indications that members of the party were becoming uneasy at signs that Young Englandism was developing a presence out-of-doors that was beyond their influence.[6]

II *Young England's Origins*

The name 'Young England' is sometimes traced to a taunt made by the ageing philosophical radical Joseph Hume in the House of Commons in July 1843 (Faber 1987, pp. 44–5) but the phrase had, in fact, been current for some time before this exchange. Disraeli applied the term to Manners and Smythe in 1841, and Milnes and his associates described themselves as 'Young Englanders' in 1837 (Disraeli 1989, p. 360; Reid 1890, pp. 205–6). From late 1842, however, 'Young England' became a public phenomenon whose parliamentary manifestations were invariably identified with Disraeli and his younger associates.

Manners traced the party's origins to August 1840. At that time he and Cochrane made unsuccessful efforts to raise a subscription to salvage the *Courier*, a floundering Tory newspaper, to serve as a flagship of their political and social views (Disraeli 1989, p. 359, n. 1). In its turn, this attempt built upon close personal interaction between Manners and his school and college friends (Lamington 1906, pp. 163–4). At Eton and Cambridge in the later 1830s and during vacations spent with the Revd Frederick Faber in the Lake District, Manners, Smythe and other Young Englanders formulated the ideas that became synonymous with their party.

Faber's impact on the impressionable Manners and Smythe was profound. In his company they refined the idea of youthful endeavour supported by intense personal friendship into a creed, and were duly rewarded by seeing their endorsement of these values praised in Faber's poetic publications.[7] Manners and Smythe also absorbed much of the tone of Faber's Tractarianism.[8] By 1838 when they had pledged themselves to a vague yet emotionally powerful quest – 'to restore what? I hardly know – but still it is a glorious attempt' (Whibley 1925, I, p. 66) – Manners and Smythe had adopted Faber's Anglo-Catholic suspicion of eighteenth-century Anglicanism. From this time they were determined to replace it with a faith the colour and warmth of which would banish the drab rationalism that they identified with the recent tradition of a misnamed 'Mother Church' (Chandler 1970, pp. 161–2).

The revival of authentic religious sentiment and a reinvigoration of the Church's social role were central to Young England's mission and had an important impact on its understanding of the broader context in which this mission was placed. Young England championed patriarchal order, admired the Stuarts and criticized liberal social and political values. For example, Smythe thought that the restoration of the Church of England as a 'true hierarchy' would provide an effective bulwark against those forces in modern society that were 'sapping and modernising all good old prejudices'. In *England's Trust and Other Poems* (1841), Manners lamented the Reformation because it had produced 'the countless sects that rend/Our once united isle from end to end' with 'their jarring and discordant sounds'. He also claimed that it had set the groundwork for unnatural ideas of human independence: 'Trace the connextion that is clearly seen/The natural parent and the State between,/And see how evenly, when men began/To slight the symbol, they unkinged the man' (Manners 1841, pp. 6, 31; below, p. 127). The time was now ripe for a revival of traditional attitudes to religion and to the Church – 'So now the purer faith of purer days/Peeps through the mould that hides the good old ways' – and for the system of political order which corresponded to them (ibid., p. 14).

But while the ideas that became identified with the Young England party in the mid-1840s were developed by its members before their political association with Disraeli began,[9] his literary reputation, parliamentary experience and steely determination to confront Peel made him an essential member of the party. Moreover, the first part of Disraeli's Young England trilogy, *Coningsby* (1844), helped to crystallize the self-image of the group, and projected its personnel and ideas onto the national stage (Faber 1987, p. 160). Two characters in this novel stood out as embodiments of Young England, Sydney who is usually identified with Manners, and Coningsby himself, who, as his sister-in-law later acidly remarked, 'panegyrised' Smythe (Strangford 1875, p. xiii).

Manners' lineage sat easily with his idealized image of a chivalrous aristocracy committed to Christian ideals, paternal responsibility and the disinterested pursuit of virtue. At Bevoir Castle, Manners' family home, and seat of the Duke of Rutland, the traditions of paternalism and deference were sustained on a splendid scale. The Duke of Rutland was a conscientious and sympathetic Poor Law Guardian. He also enjoyed the affectionate respect of his dependants. When visiting Bevoir in 1838 Charles Greville was struck by the 'loud shouts of joy and congratulations' that rang around the servants hall: 'one hundred and forty five retainers had just done dinner and were drinking the Duke's health, singing and speechifying with vociferous applause, shouting and clapping of hands' (Greville 1885, I, pp. 44–5). Manners' understanding of the role of the aristocracy was affected by his early absorption in the writings of Sir Walter Scott, and particularly by Kenelm Digby's *Broad Stone of Honour* (1829). In Digby's extraordinary work chivalry was presented as a necessary feature of beneficial human interaction, one whose potentialities had been 'infinitely ennobled' by the influence of traditional, Roman Catholic religion: 'Chivalry is only a name for that general spirit or state of mind which disposes men to heroic and generous actions, and keeps them conversant with all that is beautiful and sublime in the intellectual and moral world' (Digby 1877, I, p. 109). Digby did not think that chivalry was the exclusive preserve of the nobility, although he allowed that this spirit might be enhanced by the 'outward splendour' of aristocracy (I, p. 251). However, he stressed that the trappings of nobility were of no value unless they were supported by those forms of religious expression which had encouraged the medieval aristocracy to act chivalrously towards the lower orders (IV, pp. 78–81). Digby contrasted the conduct of ancient aristocracy with that of the 'proud, artificial, or legal nobility' of the post-Reformation world. Since elites had abandoned the true faith, they had used power selfishly, treated the poor with disdainful arrogance and set up barriers to social interaction that extended from recreation to worship (I, pp. 261–70).

Digby's writings are a rich source of Young England themes, and Manners, in particular, exemplified the desire to recover the almost extinct 'principles of loyalty and generosity' that had inspired Digby (Holland 1919, p. 81). Chivalric ideals were combined with those derived from Tractarianism to infuse absolutism with beauty, warmth and a high-toned sense of moral commitment.[10] With the help of Robert Southey's writings Manners linked these principles with the Anglican tradition and applied the values of the past to the problems of the present (see below, pp. 76–88).

Manners' causes were easy targets of ridicule but they gained some protection from the barbs of satire because of his striking looks, high-mindedness and debonair dress. Manners had the unusual distinction of being earnest *and* engaging. However, his prosaic political career and his conduct in the 1840s demonstrate that he was something more than an attractive symbol of Young England sentiment. He was active in parliamentary debates and on select committees, he promoted the Young England cause in mass meetings in the industrial north and midlands, and went to considerable lengths to prepare carefully argued and researched cases in support of such ethereal objectives as the restoration of 'national holy days' and the establishment of monastic orders in large urban centres (see below, pp. 68–87).

Disraeli venerated Manners, but he seems to have been swept away by Smythe. A quarter of a century after the end of Young England, when Smythe was long dead, Disraeli was still entranced: 'George Smythe . . . was a man of brilliant gifts; of dazzling wit, infinite culture, and fascinating manners. His influence over youth was remarkable, and he could promulgate a new faith with graceful enthusiasm' (Disraeli 1870, p. xiii). Like Manners, Smythe conjured up chivalric images to inspire his coarsened contemporaries, but in his life and writings there is an undercurrent of dangerous gallantry that contrasts sharply with the chaste earnestness of Manners' medieval yearnings. Having threatened to 'call out' an opponent in his first election campaign in 1841, Smythe incurred the censure of the Speaker of the·House of Commons for challenging John Roebuck in 1844. During his final foray into electoral politics in 1851 Smythe fought the last duel in England. To his father's disgust Smythe pursued disenchanted married women rather than the heiresses whose fortunes would have restored the financial position of his family. Smythe said that he found the role of a 'clever adventurer . . . less distasteful than the hellish bond of English matrimony' (Fonblanque 1878, p. 228). Among his *Historic Fancies* were appreciative observations on the women of the French court – 'Madame de Montespan was gifted with that rarest of beauties – light hair, with dark black eyes and eye lashes' (Smythe 1844, p. 35 n.) – and in an unguarded comment to Disraeli he indulged in rakish jests that recalled the loose moral tone of the Regency: 'My life . . . is made up of Cafés, whores, headaches, and sentiment . . . . Some day or other, when my thought develops, we ought to write a comedy together . . . . It would *pay* well & . . . it must be pleasant to hear oneself *Clapped*, who are used to another sense of that term!' (Disraeli 1989, p. 208 n. 1).

There was, moreover, a dark side to Smythe's gallantry. His alleged sexual mistreatment of a daughter of the Earl of Orford and his mercurial exhaltation and denigration of women – Sir William Gregory recalled that 'I have heard him pouring out his whole soul in ecstasies over some woman, and then . . . turn around and roll her in the mud' (Fonblanque 1878, p. 238 n. 1) – pointed to tensions in his character that were revealed in other settings. The surviving correspondence between Smythe and his father is marked by precociousness of expression and by a painful combination of assertiveness, deep affection and self-recrimination. Smythe had a penchant for what Fonblanque terms 'moral self-vivisection'(ibid., p. 214). Although this operation often gave rise to bitterness of spirit and savage self-criticism it did not produce any regularity of conduct. Smythe's lack of self-discipline was felt most strongly in his personal life, but his acute consciousness of it also hampered his political career. Despite developing a sophisticated interest in international affairs, Smythe was unable to take advantage of the opportunities presented by his appointment as an Under-Secretary at the Foreign Office under Peel in late 1845. He thus endured the agonies of having deserted his friends without reaping any benefits from it.[11]

These personal travails give a tragic air to Smythe's life but do little to vindicate the judgement that he was a 'splendid failure' (Strangford 1875, p. xxix). This verdict is plausible, however, if one takes account of Smythe's writings. In a number of elegant and witty essays Smythe exhibited a well-informed and sophisticated understanding of English and French political and literary history, and advanced a conception of politics that added an original and distinctive dimension to Young England. As noted below, Smythe endorsed his friends' perception of English political history and was at one with them on a number of issues of contemporary political importance. At the same time, however, his views on political culture rested on an ideal of 'grandeur' that was more ideologically complex than the conventional stress on nobility of spirit that played a central role in Manners' political thinking. These considerations, perhaps reinforced by the sympathy felt by one who had recently left a dandyish youth behind, may explain why the far from conventional author of *Coningsby* gave Smythe the title role in the first part of his Young England trilogy.

III *Young England as a Party*

In parliament Young England was more like a 'squadron' of the reign of Queen Anne, or a modern 'ginger group' than a conventional party of the early Victorian period. Its character was due in part to its odd structure: it was made up of a core group of members, supported by others who had not been privy to the agreement by which it was formed. This agreement was, in any case, an ambiguous one. Smythe who was with Disraeli in Paris when the party was formed and acted as the go-between, actually brokered two agreements. The agreement between Smythe, Manners and Disraeli pledged members of the party to sit together, to vote as the 'majority decides' and to consider overtures involving offers of office by 'council of ourselves'. By contrast the agreement with Cochrane ('the Celt') was, as Smythe acknowledged, 'more general and reserved': members of the group would sit together 'in the hope that association might spawn party'. This piece of double-dealing was designed to placate Cochrane's jealousy of Smythe's role in the negotiations and his resentment of Disraeli's intrusion upon relationships based on long-standing friendship.[12] At the same time, however, it reflected divergent views on the role and policy of Young England. All members of the group were disillusioned with the ethos of contemporary politics and were prepared to challenge Sir Robert Peel and his ministers when this seemed necessary. Except in the case of Disraeli, however, Young England did not see itself as an opposition within the party. As Cochrane later observed, and as their speeches and writings show, 'Young Englanders were not supposed to adopt a factious line: they simply expressed in bright and vigorous language fresh political views, which they hoped to see adopted by the Government . . .' (Lamington 1906, pp. 173–4). Even Smythe, who entered with apparent relish on the task of 'vexing and bullying' Peel, justified the establishment of Young England by reference to the need to 'animate the country party into pluck' and to '*give nerve to disaffection*'.[13]

In the early stages of its parliamentary career Young England presented a united front on Irish policy, voting against the government in 1843 on Smith O'Brien's motion and on the Irish Arms Bill.[14] These votes irritated both Peel and, somewhat ironically, the Queen as well, but they drew attention to the group and established its presence on the parliamentary scene (Faber 1987, p. 130). By the time Young England was coming to an end, however, Irish issues caused a major division within the group, most notably in votes on the grant to the Roman Catholic seminary at Maynooth (18 April 1845) and on the Irish Coercion Bill of 1846. Even in its heyday, Young England had not adhered to a common position on all issues. There was general support for Manners' protestations in support of Don Carlos in February 1844, and for Ferrand's numerous assaults upon the principles and practice of the system of poor relief introduced as a result of the Poor Law Amendment Act of 1834 (see below). On two of the major issues of the period, factory legislation and the repeal of the Corn Laws, the group recorded split votes. Manners' promotion of the Ten Hours' Bill failed to win Smythe over to a cause that he thought would weaken an important sector of the economy. More damagingly, Smythe, a consistent supporter of the principle of free trade, joined Milnes (who had never shared Manners' and Disraeli's antipathy towards Peel) in supporting the repeal of the Corn Laws in 1846. By this time, Manners had reservations about arguments in favour of protection. He sided with Peel's Conservative opponents, however, because he thought the Prime Minister should defend his new position before the electorate before attempting to reverse his party's position in a vote in the House of Commons ([Mennel] 1872, p. 81; see below, pp. 143–9).

Even before the Corn Law issue was pushed to a conclusion in Parliament, Young England's voting record would have proved fatal to any group which aspired to become a conventional party. However, Disraeli and his associates did not see themselves in this light. In the first place, as noted above, the group do not seem to have had any ambitions to form a distinct party in the conventional sense. Manners was quite emphatic about this and warned members of the parliamentary party to be wary of being drawn into a general movement. For example, at the end of 1844 he was reluctant to attend a dinner being organized by Ferrand and others in Wakefield because, as he put it in a letter to Disraeli, 'such a step savours too much of popularity hunting; the meeting has no object but to laud us, and we by sanctioning it would at once separate ourselves as a distinct political party, which I for one are not prepared to do'.[15] Secondly, both within Parliament and in its extra-parliamentary manifestations, Young Englanders were scornful of party, thinking of themselves as purveyors of non-partisan cures for the country's ills. Young England did not accept that the injection of a new, fresh, national spirit into a vapid and uninspiring political culture required programmatic uniformity or conventional party discipline. Rather, the party was seen a product of its members' commitment to a distinctive ethos.

IV *Youth, Feeling and Imagination in Politics*

Young England prided itself on the purity of its motives and was determined to remain aloof from the complacent and sordid political mainstream. Its members believed that their youth trumped the uninspiring expertise of Peel and justified their challenges to him. Decades after Young England, Cochrane recalled how refreshing it had been to pose an alternative to what he called 'the hard practical dogmatic speeches of the old *habitués*, the red-tapist

MOSES AND SON ATTIRING YOUNG ENGLAND.

THE novel of Coningsby clearly discloses
The pride of the world are the children of MOSES.
Mosaic, the bankers—the soldiers, the sailors,
The statesmen—and so, by-the-by, are the tailors.
Mosaic, the gold—that is worthless and hollow ;
Mosaic, the people—the bailiffs that follow.
The new generation—the party that claim
To take to themselves of Young England the name ;
In spite of their waistcoats much whiter than snow,
It seems after all are the tribe of Old Clo !
Then where in the world can Young England repair
To purchase the garments it wishes to wear—
Unless to that mart whose success but discloses
The folly of man, and the cunning of MOSES ?

'Cartoon for the Merchants Tailors.' *Punch*'s illustration and doggerel hit at youth and dandyism, hint of manipulation by Disraeli and play the anti-Semitic card against him and Young England. (*From the Alexander Turnbull Library, National Library of New Zealand, Te Puna Mātauranga o Aotearoa*, ref no. S-L 191.)

parliamentarians . . . . It was not like Columbus, the Old World seeking the New; it was the New World of ideas starting forth to influence, if not to renew, the Old'(Lamington 1906, pp. 153–4, 165).

Young England's devotion to the cult of youth had a mixed reception. Fellow-travellers such as Frederick Faber embraced the idea with enthusiasm, and it also struck a chord with less closely engaged commentators (see below, pp. 177–8). In some other quarters, the party was the subject of restrained and generally good-natured satire. When not indulging its taste for anti-Semitism at Disraeli's expense, *Punch* had more innocent fun with the image of fresh-faced, white waistcoated youngsters. The *virtú* of youth also provoked gentle mockery from the veteran Whig orator T. B. Macaulay. In response to Milnes' claim that an appreciation of the evils wrought by the Protestant ascendancy in Ireland was the gift of youthful insight, Macaulay declined to genuflect before the 'authority' of 'venerable youth' (see below, p. 157). Both Manners and Smythe had to withstand paternal censure, some of which sprang from distrust of Disraeli's influence upon his youthful colleagues, although these misgivings were eased by the highly favourable national reception given to the group's speeches at the opening of the Manchester Athenaeum in 1844 (Fonblanque 1878, p. 224). Other critics were less forgiving: they charged the group with arrogantly ascribing novelty and virtue to ignorance, inexperience and irresponsibility. As a leader writer in the *Morning Herald* put it, as 'that tomfoolery [Young England] is the political offshoot of Tractarianism, mental dandyism is its chief characteristic'.[16]

The fact that Milnes' appeal to the judgement of youth occurred in a debate on Irish affairs is significant. Young England claims concerning the sympathetic feelings revealed to the pure eye of youthful enthusiasm appeared with a singular clarity in their comments on Irish policy. With the exception of Ferrand, whose staunch Protestantism set him apart from his colleagues on Irish issues, Young Englanders consistently promoted conciliation as the key to a just and effective Irish policy. They urged the House to abandon its traditional hostility to the Roman Catholic Church in Ireland, expressed admiration for the character of the Irish people and insisted on the need to take full account of their feelings and to acknowledge past injustices to them (see below, pp. 101–5). For example, in early July 1843, Cochrane warned the House that the

> Irish character had not been sufficiently considered. It was noble, generous, and enthusiastic, easily excited to evil, but deeply sensible of kindness. On such minds, one cold and unkind expression would inflict more pain than a long series of legislative favours would confer pleasure.[17]

Young England thought that Irish policy had been bedevilled by the failure of English Protestants to grasp the nature of the bond that attached the Irish peasantry to their priests. This want of understanding had given rise to a pattern of administration that was at best lifelessly ineffectual, and at worst systematically unjust. As Milnes put it of the emancipation of Roman Catholics in 1829: 'the Irish Catholics were received into their rights by Act of Parliament and not by the heart of the nation' (Milnes 1844b, p. 18). Young England sought to foster attitudes that would ensure that mutual antagonism, misunderstanding and incomprehension gave way to a relationship based on sympathy, deference and a shared sense of identity. Since these qualities were associated with ideas of feudal dependence, aspects of Young England's Irish policy mirrored those advanced by conservative members of 'Young Ireland'. Like them, Young Englanders thought that the baleful effect of religious sectarianism had been exacerbated by the mechanical and utilitarian cast of the modern English mind.[18]

Young England's sympathy for the Irish reflected a perception that, in common with the peasantry in isolated areas of France and Spain, they were more capable of embodying values of piety, simplicity and deference than the spiritually debased masses of industrial and urban England. In all these cases, however, a central role was ascribed to the Church (Manners 1840, pp. 577–9, 111; see below, pp. 68–93). Young England's support for the Roman Catholic Church in Ireland was a consequence of the belief that as the 'church of the people' this institution should be placed in a position to assume the responsibilities that they were urging the Anglican Church to fulfil with regard to the lower classes in England. In both cases the aim was to incorporate excluded or marginalized sections of the population within the national community.

On one level, Young England's conciliatory Irish policy echoed the line taken by the Whig administration in the late 1830s (Gray 1992, pp. 15–16). It rested, however, upon distinctive assumptions about the role of imagination and sympathy in politics, and was part of a larger argument about the social and political importance of religion that differed sharply from the ideas about civil and religious liberty that underwrote Whig policy. These differences in perception were quite apparent in the appeals to history made by the Whigs, on the one hand, and Young England on the other. While the Whigs evoked the name of Charles James Fox (ibid., pp. 29–30), Young England looked back to the younger Pitt and to George Canning. These men were the most recent parts of what was, in effect, a new history of Anglo-Irish relationships, one that focused upon worthy, but frustrated, attempts to treat the Irish justly and to struggle against the triumphant but poisonous legacy of extreme Protestantism. In this history Charles I, Strafford, James II, Pitt and Canning were the heroes, and Cromwell, William of Orange and the eighteenth-century Whigs were the villains.

V The 'Condition of England Question'

For Manners and his colleagues, the political significance of sympathetic feeling was not restricted to Anglo-Irish affairs. Rather, it was a central tenet of their ethos, one that lay at the heart of their criticism of contemporary religious attitudes[19] and also played an important role in their initiatives on behalf of the English working classes. Like many of their contemporaries, Young Englanders were uneasy about the social and moral impact of rapid industrialization, particularly when this was accompanied by calls, from both philosophic radicals and 'liberal' Tories such as Peel, for the abandonment of paternalistic conceptions of government (Hilton 1988).

In a highly favourable review of *Sybil*, Disraeli was complimented for having identified 'mammon-worship' as the key to the social and moral evils that afflicted the lower classes (see below, p. 33). The worship of this false idol displaced the regard for human interests that was central to Christianity, and it also gave rise, as Ferrand put it, to a 'gambling spirit' that destabilized commercial life (see below, p. 49). In pursuit of what Cochrane later described as Young England's 'great objective', securing relief for the working classes from the 'tyranny of manufactures and employers', both he and Manners promoted legislation regulating the hours and conditions of factory workers (Lamington 1906, p. 151, and see below, pp. 63–5). The party also furnished trenchant critiques of the 'new' Poor Law of 1834. With Ferrand in the van, Young England harried the government on a number of related issues, particularly the use of the power of Poor Law guardians to sweep paupers from rural unions into an unregulated manufacturing sector.[20] Manners' opposition to the Poor Law extended to the very idea of a state-administered system of poor relief: 'the administration of the funds for the maintenance of the poor ought to be in the hands of the Church'.[21] Manners and Ferrand were also to the forefront of attempts to enact allotment schemes in the expectation that they would lessen the dependence of factory workers on irregular wage labour, instil in them a sense of dignity and (suitably grateful) independence, and restore a much-needed step in the social hierarchy. They established 'cottage gardens' in their own neighbourhoods, encouraged their friends to follow suit,[22] sat on a Commons Committee investigating the value of allotments[23] and promoted legislation that would supplement private initiatives (see below, pp. 60–2).

But while Young England threw its weight behind attempts to alleviate the moral degradation and unnecessary material hardship suffered by industrial workers in the midlands and north of England, the group was not opposed to industrial progress. To the contrary, in widely reported speeches delivered at the opening of the Manchester Athenaeum in 1844, members of the party took a positive line on the achievements of modern industry. Disraeli emphasized this feature of Young England's position in passages in *Coningsby* that portrayed a character that was modelled closely upon Smythe.[24] In his writings, Smythe wrote warmly of the liberal economic heritage of Bolingbroke, Pitt and Canning, saw grandeur in the process of industrial development and painted merchant venturers in heroic colours. By contrast, Manners' positive remarks on industrial society were premised on the assumption that the relationships between workers and their employers might embody values associated with pre-industrial society. On a visit to a model cotton factory in Lancashire in 1842, Manners noted with approval that the proprietor was a 'modern lord, having, in fact, an absolute dominion over his men'. There was, he later commented, 'never . . . so complete a feudal system as that of the mills; soul and body are, or might be, at the absolute disposal of one man, and that to my notion is not at all a bad state of society'.[25] The real evil of the modern factory system was that it generally combined complete dependence with uncertainty of employment, irresponsibility on the part of employers, neglect by the Church and indifference by a state that had abandoned its paternal responsibilities.

VI   The Social Role of the Church

Support for factory legislation and allotment schemes and criticism of the new Poor Law were not, as a critic in *Fraser's Magazine* pointed out, novel responses to the 'Condition of England' problem (see below, pp. 181–2). However, the ethos of Young England allowed the group to present these issues in a distinctive light. In addition, Manners pursued idiosyncratic ways of ensuring the restoration of what he took to be a proper sense of elite responsibility and of beneficial interaction between different classes. The key to realizing these aspirations lay in a variety of arrangements designed to ensure that social relationships were mediated by a truly *national* church. Manners urged the Church to abandon its detached post-Laudian stance and to reassume its place as the focal point of a revived sense of national identity and social membership.

One set of Manners' prescriptions focused on the Church's role as a director of the lives of the working classes and as a source of psychological, spiritual and material support. In rural areas, these offices could be performed adequately by parish clergy, but the deprived and demoralized state of a large and rapidly growing urban population called for less conventional measures. Manners juxtaposed images of the 'monastic' and 'manufacturing' systems,[26] in order to make a case for establishing monastic institutions in urban centres to supplement church-building programmes and to facilitate working-class participation in Anglican services (see below, pp. 76–87). By gathering clergymen together under a common roof the human and material resources of the Church would be concentrated. Members of new, Protestant monastic orders (not bound by vows and subject to the authority of bishops) would support one another's efforts to provide leadership and comfort to the working classes.

Manners' favourable references to medieval monastic institutions, and Young England's tolerant attitude to the Roman Catholic Church in Ireland, prompted accusations of sympathy for 'popery'. In response, Manners stressed that his way of thinking had an impeccable Protestant pedigree. He also insisted, as did some of his colleagues, that since the Church had been damaged by its dependence on a parsimonious state, it was futile to look for government support for the Church (see below, pp. 86–7). The Church's resources should be augmented by charitable donations from its wealthier members; this would only be possible, however, if the 'Mortmain Statutes' were repealed.[27]

This term referred to a number of sixteenth-, seventeenth- and eighteenth-century legislative enactments curtailing individuals' rights to leave landed property to the Church (see below, pp. 88–93). Manners argued that the repeal of these statutes would ensure that the Church acquired the means necessary to fulfil its traditional role as the material and spiritual guide and comforter of the lower orders. In so doing, it would become the conduit through which the charitable energy released by Christianity could be brought to bear on the destabilizing enthralment of modern society to the accumulation of wealth.

Following Robert Southey, Manners attributed this tendency to the triumph of Calvinistic impulses in post-Laudian Anglicanism. He maintained that the perversion of Protestantism had resulted in the neglect of the poor's claims both to charitable relief and to provisions for innocent and invigorating recreations. Such proposals were not uncommon in the 1840s,[28] but Manners took a distinctive Young England approach to the issue, proposing a campaign to restore the 'holy-days' that had provided regular refreshment for the labouring classes in pre-industrial England. He saw this step as a necessary companion-piece to the restriction of work hours in factories. The working classes needed relief from remorseless toil, but Manners insisted that 'holy-days' were not mere holidays: they were noted in the traditional calendar of the Church and combined recreation with religious observances. Holy-days were also valuable because they provided opportunities for interaction between classes that would reduce the impact of great inequalities of wealth. Manners looked forward to a time when 'the lusty apprentice shall not fear to overleap his master's son, nor the pauper's heir to contend with the guardian's brother' (see below, p. 69). The reintegration of the Church within the life of the community was central to this vision:

> She it is, and she only, that can knit together in the sanctifying bands of Christian joy and sorrow, Christian fast and festival, the high and the low, the rich and the poor; – she it is, and she only, that can bless the enslaving toil of the husbandman or the craft of the mechanic, on earth, with glimpses of heaven.

It was by these means, and not by the inappropriate and unrealistic extension of intellectual culture from the middle to the lower classes, that the 'frankness and good humour, the strength and the glory of the good old English character' would be restored, and the 'thoughts of discontent and moroseness' that had left large sections of society prey to beguiling but false attractions of chartists and socialists would be purged from the English mind (see below, pp. 134–5).

VII   *The Creation of a National Political Culture: Party, Aristocracy and Monarchy*

Although Manners' emphasis upon the Church's role was far more emphatic than that of other Young Englanders, the difference was one of degree rather than of kind. Even in Manners' case, the demand that the Church reaffirm its role as 'the church of the people' had to be understood in relation to a broader concern with revitalizing the political culture of contemporary England. That is, Manners thought that the influence of religion should be brought to bear in politics rather than displacing it.

The ideal of political culture promoted by Young England was defined in part by its reaction to undesirable features of the contemporary social and political environment. Both within Parliament and in the extra-parliamentary movement, Young England figures bewailed the shackles imposed upon honest and imaginative political endeavour by anti-national, mechanical and unworthy notions of party, and they resisted the malign combination of arrogant parliamentary manipulation and cool administrative expertise that they identified with Peel and his allies. Anti-party sentiments were directed at both major parties, but they were premised upon claims about the Whigs' baleful influence on the recent political history of England. This critique originated in Disraeli's claim that the Whigs had transformed constitutional monarchy into a 'Venetian' oligarchy (Disraeli 1836, pp. 184–94, and see below, p. 53). Manners embellished Disraeli's account by exploring the harmful effects of Dutch finance and Dutch Calvinism on the tone of English political culture and on public taste, noting the impact of these alien forces in such diverse fields as religious observance in England, and the civic and ecclesiastical architecture of Dublin (Manners 1881, pp. 3–5, 9, 21). Smythe's accounts of eighteenth-century politics were coloured by other variants upon the Disraelian theme. For example, he lauded Bolingbroke's critique of Walpole's administrations, and congratulated him on trying to forge an alliance between a truly national aristocracy and the common people (Smythe 1844, p. 138).

Young England maintained that oligarchic corruption and the insidious growth of commercial culture had undermined monarchy and aristocracy, and it sought to restore these institutions to their rightful forms. In a manner reminiscent of figures in early German Romanticism, Young Englanders tried to reclaim the centre of the political stage for monarchy by reclothing it in the glorious hues of traditional, chivalric kingship (Beiser 1996, pp. 35–41). They idealized at least the form of absolute monarchy, glanced nostalgically at the history of the Stuarts and condemned those who had cruelly misused these models of royal dignity. Smythe admired Bolingbroke's 'patriot king' and wrote enthusiastically of the mystical beauty of the now discarded tradition of 'touching for evil' by the monarch: this 'graceful superstition' had produced 'direct communication between the highest and the lowest' (Smythe 1844, p. 91; below, p. 129). Young England treatments of monarchy were not just historically based homilies: both Disraeli and Smythe sought to identify qualities in the young Queen Victoria which had escaped the attention of their contemporaries (Disraeli 1845, Bk IV, ch. 14; below, p. 132). These ideas on kingship were endorsed by Manners, who saw a modern candidate for royal martyrdom in Don Carlos of Spain, a victim of the 'sacrilegious spirit of modern liberalism' (Whibley 1925, I, p. 167).

Young England regarded an effective monarch as the focal point of a patriarchal regime in which aristocracy should have a significant role. Members of the group associated the tarnished image of modern monarchy with a corrupt aristocratic ethos that had emerged in the late seventeenth and eighteenth centuries. Manners' accounts of aristocracy stressed its social rather than its constitutional responsibilities. In *England's Trust* the 'old nobility' appear as links in a chain of responsive hierarchy that began with the monarch and ended with 'peasantry' and other members of the lower orders (see below, pp. 115–17). It is important to note that Manners used the idea of an 'old nobility' as a moral rather than a purely historical category. The 'old nobility' stood in a special relationship with its dependants, and in order to remain true to their order, present members of the aristocracy must give reality to their social and political position. They should thus protect the interests of those who were connected to them personally, and bring a more general paternal influence to bear in national politics. As a self-conscious member of the old nobility, Manners took both of these facets of aristocratic responsibility very seriously. He therefore promoted practical improvements on his father's extensive estates (and was mortified, as well as being embarrassed politically, when alleged mistreatment of cottagers by one of the Duke of Rutland's agents was brought to his attention[29]) and argued the case for legislative paternalism in the House of Commons.

Smythe's published comments on aristocracy were far more complex than those of Manners and tended to emphasize the contribution that the nobility could make to the tone of particular political cultures. In *Historic Fancies* Smythe dwelt at length on the history of the French aristocracy, contrasting the arrogant, self-willed but public-spirited ancient aristocracy with the pampered ingrates who were raised to noble status by Louis XV and his successors (see below, pp. 117–23). This aristocracy had played an important role in preparing the way for the French Revolution of 1789, but Smythe speculated that their chastening experiences during the revolutionary and post-revolutionary periods might have encouraged them to resume their traditional role as servants and supporters of a monarchical state. In Smythe's writings, the drama and tragedy of English aristocracy cannot compare with that of its French cousins. Even in this case, however, the same pattern can be seen: the debasement of aristocracy by Charles II yielding its treacherous and tragic fruits in his brother's reign (see below, pp. 128–9).

The ambivalence of Smythe's treatment of the recent history of aristocracy is reinforced by his endorsement of Bolingbroke's idea of a 'Patriot King' beset by a self-serving pseudo-aristocratic oligarchy.[30] But while critical of the pretensions of the courtiers and 'nobles of the robe' who had been elevated into the upper reaches of the aristocracy since the Glorious Revolution, Smythe had no intention of undermining aristocratic influence in English politics. Rather, his object seems to have been to uphold a distinctive and pure conception of the ethos of aristocracy in the face of developments that threatened to debase it. Aristocracies became redundant only when they were incapable of giving a distinctive tone to social and political life.

VIII *Conclusion*

Young England's wish to redefine the role of aristocracy and to reintegrate it with monarchy was part of a larger attempt to establish a national culture as the basis for political thought and action. This programme required the creation (or, in Young England's view, the recovery) of attitudes to elite leadership that were conducive to social cohesion and to communal well-being. It also necessitated the elimination of political and religious partisanship and the blind pursuit of class or sectional interests. These practices fragmented society and deprived the poor in England and Roman Catholics in Ireland of the benefits of membership of the community.

The pursuit of an ideal of national community gave a degree of coherence to the various elements in the Young England programme, and explained its responses to the Condition of England question as well as its ideas on political and social culture. Young England promoted solutions to the Condition of England question that sought to alleviate unnecessary hardship by creating the basis for a sense of common identity. They were thus critical of their contemporaries' disregard for feeling and imagination because this deprived members of the community of sympathy with their fellows. Consequently, members of the movement extolled the virtues of the historical 'churches of the people' – Anglican in England; Roman Catholic in Ireland, France and Spain. These churches remained faithful to conceptions of Christianity that encouraged communal sympathy, and gave concrete expression to this idea in the pastoral role ascribed to the priesthood. Young England thought that a revival of popular culture would produce related benefits. When traditional sports and pastimes were supervised by participating elites, and took place on days that were both *holy* and *national*, they drew classes together and provided a common focus for an important aspect of their lives. They became manifestations of a sense of national culture that corresponded with Manners' conception of the true history of a nation: 'the history of . . . the habits, thoughts, and tastes of its people'(Whibley 1925, I, p. 177).

But while Young England's writings were steeped in the past, it sought to promote an inclusive ideal that incorporated progressive forces. For this reason, Young England writers tried to engage with the middle classes of the industrial north and resisted attempts to drive a wedge between the industrial and landed interests. Young England's commitment to what French Romantics called 'social politics' was addressed to the working classes, but middle-class confidence meant that this class posed a rather different challenge to attempts to incorporate it within a national culture. Young England attempted to meet this challenge by moving tentatively towards a broad and progressively inclined ideal in which the middle class could find an honourable place. Thus in his speech to the Manchester Athenaeum, Manners applauded its members' growing interest in history, architecture and the fine arts, while Smythe, with characteristic panache, portrayed Manchester as the seat of a renaissance in letters that would eventually match the achievements of the Italian city states.

Finally, it should be noted that whatever role ambition, pique or the wish for excitement or for notoriety played in Young England's harrying of Peel, the party's parliamentary stance was consistent with its general position. Many of Peel's reforming and liberalizing initiatives were motivated by his determination to insulate the machinery of government from the influence of self-concerned sectional interests (Hilton 1988, pp. 230–1). Young England was more alarmed at the way in which this objective was pursued than with the goal itself. By dragging its feet on Irish issues and factory legislation, and by spurning Young England's pet projects, Peel's government demonstrated to the group that it lacked the vision necessary to undertake an effective system of national administration. Moreover, from a Young England perspective, there was much more at stake in the battle over the Corn Laws in 1845–6 than the continuation of agricultural protection. By his high-handed and manipulative treatment of the landed interest within his party, Peel undermined its standing in the eyes of the community. In so doing, he exhibited an attitude towards politics that was antithetical to Young England's idea of the role that aristocracy should play in a revived national culture.

Notes to the Introduction

1. Accusations of oligarchy, and claims about the harmful effects of 'Dutch finance', together with attempts to restore Lord Bolingbroke's reputation, provide links with the tradition of Country Party argument, first developed in response to Sir Robert Walpole's administrations; see Pocock 1974, chs 11–12.

2. For an account of Disraeli's conception of his ancestry see Disraeli n.d., p. 126. Alexander Baillie Cochrane (1816–90) was created first Baron Lamington in 1880. His grandfather was the younger son of the eighth Earl of Dundonald. Lord John Manners (1818–1906), second son of the fifth Duke of Rutland succeeded his brother to the title in 1888. Manners served as First Commissioner of Works, Postmaster-General and Chancellor of the Duchy of Lancaster in Conservative cabinets between 1852 and 1892. George Sydney Smythe (1818–57) succeeded his father as seventh Viscount Strangford (in the Irish peerage) and second Baron Penhurst in 1855. Smythe accepted office under Peel in late 1845 as Foreign Under-Secretary and followed Peel when he broke from the Conservative Party in June 1846.

3. Alexander Beresford-Hope (1820–87) was a politician and author with particular expertise in architecture; Peter Borthwick (1804–52) editor of the *Morning Post* from 1850; William Busfield Ferrand (1809–89) a landowner with extensive property in the neighbourhood of Bingley in Yorkshire; and Richard Monckton Milnes (1809–85) a politician and poet of note. A friend of Thomas Carlyle, Milnes left the Conservative Party with Peel in 1846 and later adopted a strongly liberal stance; he was created the first Baron Houghton in 1863.

4. Once established in the popular imagination, the idea of 'Young England' was taken up by publicists who had little or nothing in common with the positions advanced by those who comprised the parliamentary party. For example, 'Young England' was used as the pseudonym by the author of two works (*Argumentum ad Populum: Tracts for Manhood No. 1: On Seeming* (1844), and *Argumentum ad Populum: Tracts for Manhood on Regeneration, Social, Moral and Spiritual* (1845)) that are strongly anti-aristocratic and anti-formalist and sound more like Carlyle than Young England.

5. A letter designed to prompt a broader movement is printed below, pp. 41–2. See p. 9 for Manners' attitude to extra-parliamentary action. A number of references to Young England initiatives in the provinces appear in the newspaper mentioned above; it also carried an advertisement for a Young England novel: E. M. Stewart's *Rodenhurst: or, The Church and the Manor*, which extolled the 'co-operation of

wealth and rank, and learning, and good purpose, on the part of the rector and the Earl; its result was in the fair face of cultivated Nature, in the smiling faces, and light hearts of a virtuous and happy peasantry' (vol. I, p. 57).

6. There is an interesting account of the demise of the Young England Party in the pamphlet by 'A Non-Elector' (ascribed in the Bodleian catalogue to Philip Mennel). The author argues that the conversion of John Henry Newman and Frederick Faber in 1845 undermined Young England's faith in the efficacy of an 'ecclesiastical revival', while the split in the Conservative Party precluded the possibility of seeking political alternatives to it. Henceforth, the members of the group had to throw in their lot with one of the great parties; see [Mennel] 1872, pp. 71–4. In the preface to *Lothair* (1870) Disraeli stressed the impact of Newman's conversion; see Disraeli 1870, pp. xv–xvi.

7. For a very good account of Faber's impact on Young England see Faber 1987. Faber's tributes to Manners and Smythe appeared in *The Cherwell Water-Lily* and *The Styrian Lake*. In the latter, Faber wrote of Manners that 'Through good and ill/With earnest will/Thou toil'st for peer and peasant' (p. 201).

8. See Chadwick 1990 for a masterly outline of Tractarianism.

9. For a recent account that highlights the group's independent origins, see Smith 1996, p. 57.

10. Edward Copleston's comment that 'if we strip off the hide of Newman we shall find Filmer underneath' (Whibley 1925, I, p. 75) was thus both harsh and unfair. In common with French and German romantics, Young England thought that conventional absolutism was cold, mechanical and repulsive. Smythe, for example, was impressed by the grandeur of French monarchy, not by its power; see below, pp. 117–24.

11. A letter that Smythe wrote to Disraeli in 1852 indicated the pain he felt at the sense of being seen as a betrayer; Hughenden Mss, 144/1/fos 236–8, 24.2.1852.

12. Ibid., 144/1/fo. 225, Smythe to Disraeli, 14.11.1842. Cochrane's poem 'To G[eorge] S[mythe]' exemplifies his perception of the bonds that bound him, Manners and Smythe and goes some way to explaining his hostility to Disraeli: '. . . Yet dearer, far dearer than glory's bright ray,/Is the tear of affection which nothing can smother,/And nobler than even thy talent's proud sway,/Is the heart that can throb and can feel for another' (Cochrane 1841a, p. 97). There is an interesting discussion of Young England friendships in Faber 1987, pp. 63–75.

13. Hughenden Mss, 144/1/fos 227, 229, Smythe to Disraeli, 20.10.1844, Smythe's emphasis.

14. On 4 July O'Brien, MP for Limerick and a leading figure in Young Ireland, moved 'That this House will resolve itself into a committee for the purpose of taking into consideration the issues of the discontent at present prevailing in Ireland, with a view to the redress of grievances, to the establishment of a just and impartial system of government in that part of the Kingdom' (*House of Commons Debates*, 70 c630–1). The Irish Arms Bill was introduced on 28 April: it provided for the continuation of regulations governing the possession, sale and importation of arms, ammunition and gunpowder into Ireland (ibid., 68 c1011). This bill was opposed on the grounds that it failed to address the causes of discontent in Ireland.

15. Hughenden Mss, 106/1/fo. 18, Manners to Disraeli, 17.11.1844.

16. *Morning Herald*, 20 July 1843, p. 4, and see below, p. 187n22. Young England was the target of heavy-handed satire in the novel ('by an Embyro MP') entitled *Anti-Coningsby; or, The New Generation Grown Old*. When Peel is defeated over the Sugar Duties in 1844 his administration is replaced by one led by 'Coningsby', regarded by some as a 'staunch Russian; others as a ferocious Jacobin. In reality he

was neither one nor the other, but a New Englandite, i.e., a sort of cross between the two' (I, p. 69). A Young England parliament votes itself perpetual and raises 'Ben Sidonia' (Disraeli) to the position of Emperor. These measures inaugurate a period of feudal oppression. The novel is markedly anti-Semitic (Jews dominate the new peerage); it also contains some hits against Manners ('Lord Gymnastic Customs'). In a spoof on Manners' 'Holy Days' speech, he is seen proposing the restoration of *all* rights of lords of the manor, including those over newly-wed peasant women (I, pp. 155–6).

17. *House of Commons Debates*, 70 c749, 7.7.1843; below p. 102.
18. O'Brien 1843, pp. 48–9; Duffy 1890, pp. 76, 83. O'Brien corresponded with Manners on Irish matters (Hughenden Mss, 106/1/fo. 29, Manners to Disraeli, 26.11.1844).
19. For example, Baillie Cochrane traced the savage tone of anti-Catholicism to a lack of feeling: 'there are many minds which possess no instinctive love of the noble and the beautiful' (Cochrane 1841a, p. 18).
20. *House of Commons Debates*, 66 c1026–8, 20.2.1843; 66 c1221–42, 23.2.1843.
21. Ibid., 66 c1217, 23.2.1843.
22. Ward 1965–6; [Mennel] 1872, pp. 20–1. In 1873 Manners wistfully surveyed 'allotment gardens' at Matlock that had been opened by Disraeli 30 years before (Hughenden Mss, 106/3/fo. 22, Manners to Disraeli, 24.8.1873).
23. *Parliamentary Papers* (1843) VII: 'Report of the Select Committee . . . into the Allotments System . . .'; *House of Commons Debates*, 71 c185–8, 21.6.1843. In 1846 Manners was one of the promoters of 'village communities', a Christian version of some Owenite settlements. One important point of difference was that the clergy were to play a prominent role in these communities; see Chadwick 1966, p. 348.
24. Disraeli 1844, Bk I, chs 1, 4, 9. Jane Ridley (1995, pp. 276–8) stresses the impact made upon Disraeli by his experience of Manchester (for him it symbolized the 'spirit of the age'). But while these passages may well record Disraeli's views rather than Smythe's, the latter's Manchester speech makes it clear that he too regarded the city as an expression of modern grandeur (Hughenden Mss, 106/1/fo. 29, Manners to Disraeli, 26.11.1844; below, pp. 136–7).
25. Whibley 1925, I, 100, 106. Young England did not think that this dominion should be converted into political power; it is sometimes thought that Disraeli's *Coningsby* supports such a move, but see the counter argument of Clausson 1986, pp. 1–4.
26. This formulation echoed A. W. Pugin's *Contrasts; or, A Parallel Between the Noble Edifices of the Fourteenth and Fifteenth Centuries, and Similar Buildings of the Present Day; shewing The Present Decay of Taste* (1836), which was inspired by a remark made in Southey's *Sir Thomas More* (1829) and used as a motto to Manners' *Monastic and Manufacturing Systems* (see below, p. 76). Pugin's book contains a series of short chapters setting the criticism of modern architecture in the context of religious, moral and social decadence of the post-Reformation period, and contrasting it with medieval products. Accompanying plates contrast a range of edifices (churches, conduits, house fronts, educational institutions) in the medieval and modern periods, always greatly to the credit of the former. Pugin was a Roman Catholic, but many of the themes of his writings (the critique of the tone of Protestantism, the social and religious virtues of pre-Reformation societies, paternalism) were also important for Young England. Manners' remarks on ecclesiastical and civil architecture in Ireland (see Manners 1881, pp. 3, 9, 13) are reminiscent of Pugin.

27. In a debate on Manners' parliamentary resolution on this issue, Sir James Graham, the Home Secretary, turned Manners' argument back against him: 'The noble Lord entertained the opinion that it might be desireable to re-establish religious houses . . . . Now he [Graham] entreated the House . . . to pause before they passed a resolution condemning the statute of Mortmain, which imposed a salutory check upon fancies such as these' (*House of Commons Debates*, 71 c110, 1.8.1843). Sir Robert Inglis, exhibiting the sectarian narrowness that Manners deplored, supported the resolution provided that Dissenters and Roman Catholics were excluded (ibid., 71 c114).

28. For an example of an earlier statement see [Anon.] (1840) 'Ancient and Modern Ways of Charity', p. 58.

29. Hughenden Mss, 106/1/fos 17–20, Manners to Disraeli, 4.11.1844.

30. For Smythe's view of Bolingbroke see 'An Opposition Scene in the Last Century' (Smythe 1844, pp. 136–8). In 'King James the Second' (see below, p. 130). Smythe was critical of the self-interest of modern aristocracy and identified monarchs as the true friends of the people. This passage provided the basis for a critical note in an otherwise very favourable review of *Historic Fancies* in the pro-Young England *Morning Post*. The reviewer (who may have been Manners) thought that Smythe did not 'draw with sufficient clearness the distinction which he points at between a real and a *pseudo* English aristocracy'; *Morning Post*, 13 July 1844, p. 5.

Lord John Manners

*(From the Alexander Turnbull Library, National Library of New Zealand,
Te Puna Mātauranga o Aotearoa,* ref no. S-L 194.)

Young England on Young England

The texts in Part I provide a number of insights into how members of Young England understood the movement. The aristocratic ancestry of Manners and his friends formed a highly personalised framework for far-reaching claims concerning the tone of nobility and its historical and contemporary roles. In advancing these claims, members of Young England self-consciously assumed the mantle of a pure and vigorous new generation possessing a unique capacity for grasping the moral and social problems of the age and formulating solutions to them. Young England's social mission was of great importance to its extra-parliamentary supporters.

1 Friendship, Nobility and Grandeur in Politics

(i) Friendship and Nobility

Lord John Manners' and George Smythe's dedications of books and poems to each other signalled their commitment to the idea that there was a close connection between the personal friendship of young aristocrats, nobility of character and the Young England project.

Lord John Manners, 'The Meeting. To G. S. S.'[1]

IV

> . . . at Rome, while hanging o'er the tomb
>   Of those, the last of Stuart's line,
> Shrouded from gazers by the evening's gloom,
>   My sighs did yearn to melt with thine.
> For there was no one who could grieve with me,
> The lonely mourner from beyond the sea.

V

> So do I cherish half-formed hopes, that e'er
>   Our boyish spirit, with our boyish years,

> Hath fled, we two together may repair,
> To mingle at that tomb our tears,
> And pray together to the Lord in heaven,
> That our dear country's sin may be forgiven.

George Smythe, 'Dedication', *Historic Fancies*[2]

To Lord John Manners, M.P.,/Whose Gentle Blood/Is Only an Illustration of His Gentler Conduct,/And Whose Whole Life/May Well Remind Us That The Only Child of Philip Sydney Became A Manners,/Because He Is, Himself, As True And Blameless,/The Philip Sydney/Of Our/Generation.

(ii)   Conflict and Grandeur in History

George Smythe's fascination with the history of early-modern France was due to his belief that it exemplified a confrontation between sharply contrasting ideas and practices whose juxtaposition presented politics in a dramatic and exhilarating light.

George Smythe, 'Preface', *Historic Fancies*

[. . .] It is . . . not without an object, that I have referred so frequently to France. For in treating many parties and opinions, I have here been able to speak without prejudice or favour. I could here admire the genius of great men, without being called upon to share in their feuds and passions. I could here confess, without fear of misrepresentation, that I see the grandeurs of conflicting principles, that I am moved by the glorious recollections, now of the old Monarchy, now of the Revolution, now of the Empire. . . . But it was not only out of a desire to learn and speak the truth of all parties. It was natural to me, – attempting to suggest modern historical reflections, – to turn to that great people, whose recent history is a mighty panorama; – where the colouring is more brilliant, the groups more striking, the tints more varied, the contrasts more abrupt, where the light is softer, the shade more dark, than in any other which I have known. It is here that we have the most perfect [ii] theory of Absolutism. It is here that we have looked upon the most perfect theory of a Republic. It is here that the Great Compromise between the two will be the most broadly tried, most severely tested, most earnestly discussed.[iii]

2 The Idea of a 'New Generation'

Young England saw itself as being at the forefront of a 'new generation' that would infuse fresh sympathy and understanding into political practice and reflections upon it. This perception is apparent in an anonymous review of *Sybil* that provided a manifesto for literary and parliamentary Young Englandism, and in Disraeli's retrospective account of the movement.

(i) *Literature and Politics*

[Anon.], 'The Policy of the New Generation'[3]

A witty Frenchman has said that the only way to teach history in these days is through romance, and Mr. Disraeli, in *Coningsby* and *Sybil*, while portraying in the faithfulest colours the men and women, the horses and asses, the fashions and follies of his own time, has managed to insinuate into whatever understanding the novel-reading public may be supposed to possess, views of English history as novel as they are correct. In *Coningsby* the seed was sown, in *Sybil* the green plant is peering through the earth.[1] . . . Oxford and Cambridge, Eton and Manchester, Birmingham and the House of Commons – the seats of learning and the hives of industry, the emporiums of wealth and the chambers of ignorant indifference – nay, even the cottages of rustic poverty have heard the startling voice, which proclaims we have been the victims of delusion, and points to the Church and the Crown as the only hope for the people.[4] . . . Encouraged then, we may suppose by manifestations of popular sympathy, such as awaited him at Manchester and elsewhere, and relying on the evidently increasing disinclination of the people to be any longer duped by either of the heartless factions which have so long fattened on the ignorant bigotry they themselves have stimulated,[2] Mr. Disraeli has not hesitated to lay before the public, views of history and of politics, the truth of which it is the object of this Review in the main to confirm and enforce. .... [3]

... [F]or any indications on the part of this administration or the legislature which it rules with so absolute a sway, of a desire to compass those other ends which we have specified, we look in vain. '*Rem, si possis recte si non quocunque modo, rem*', seems to be the rule deliberately adopted by every leading politician in the House of Commons, with the exception of Lord Ashley, and of the 'New Generation' whose views *Sybil* may be regarded to express.[5] All measures are judged of by the consideration 'will it increase the wealth of the country?' And if a minister can show that in the present year there is more bullion in the bank, and more millions invested in railroads than in any previous year, the mammon-worshippers are in ecstasies, and the people are congratulated by the royal lips at the close of a weary session, from which they derive no possible benefit, on their flourishing and prosperous condition. Fatal delusion! The same minister who boasts of the eighty millions embarked in railway speculations yet unfinished, informs the Commons through his Poor-law Commissioners that one eighth of the people are paupers.[6] Let the country continue to flourish and [4] prosper after this fashion – let the eighty millions be doubled, and let every fourth Englishman instead of every eighth be a pauper, and what then? – a revolution, such as the world has not yet seen. The extent to which this wealth-adoration is pushed, is as ludicrous as it is alarming: it makes a liberal peer exact the last farthing for the rent of a lug of land from the starving peasant, and insists on the industry of the country being entirely dependent on money-wages; though it shrinks with horror from any attempt to secure the permanence or sufficiency of those wages. Mr. Disraeli sees the rottenness of such a system, and exposes with happiest power the sophisms and perversions of history on which it is based, and the consequences to which it is rapidly leading. The destruction of the monasteries, and the alienation of their lands from the people to the courtiers, is a favourite topic with the economic philosophers; and even Mr. Hallam is induced by his whiggery to do despite to his kindlier feelings, and defend that spoilation. The most delightful and philosophical perhaps of all the chapters in *Sybil* is devoted to an examination of Mr Hallam's dictum, 'Better has it been that those revenues should thus from age to age have been expended in liberal hospitality, in discerning charity, in the promotion of industry and cultivation, in the active duties, or even generous amusements of life, than in maintaining a host of ignorant and inactive monks, in deceiving the populace by superstitious pageantry, or in the encouragement of idleness and mendicity.'[7] . . . [5]

All classes were benefited by the monasteries; but conspicuously the poor: for poverty was by and through them, regarded throughout the Christian world as holy; poverty is now a crime, and wealth sacred. If the poor are ever again in England to regain their rights, and true position in the Christian scheme, it will be through the re-establishment of that system which fell before the cupidity of Henry. That such a re-establishment will take place we have little doubt, for the most powerful minds and ablest pens are worthily employed in bringing it about. Such remarkable works as Carlyle's *Past and Present*, Professor Sewell's papers in the *Quarterly Review*, 'Hawkstone,' and *Sybil*, can hardly fail to convince the most idolatrous worshipper of wealth, that poverty will ere long have other homes raised for it than those unsightly piles of brick and mortar which men with £1200 a year call workhouses, and the people – bastilles.[8]

In a work intended to give a faithful sketch of the present commonalty of England, it was impossible to omit altogether that remarkable feature in it – Socialism; and Mr. Disraeli has put into the mouth of the socialist, Morley, many of those denunciations of our present wealth-ridden system, which in fact were the means whereby the awful tenets of that sad materialism found an entrance into English hearts. We have heard Morley pronounced an unnatural conception; we, on the contrary, hold him to be a very exact specimen of those clever, insinuating and totally vicious and unprincipled men, who taking advantage of the diseased state of social life, hold out to the thirsty and despairing lips of toil and want the drugged chalice of sensual delight. . . . To the miserable peasant (or agricultural labourer as it is now [7] the fashion to call him, perhaps 'foot' will soon be his appellation as a parallel to the manufacturing 'hand') shivering in his cheerless hut with half-starved peevish children around him, without one ray of hope of ever rising out of his present misery, with the Union-shell the last object visible to his contracted sight, how full of hope and happiness must sound the glowing descriptions of a community of goods, and an equality of labour! To him sighing over the destruction of an English home, comes the subtle whisper of the socialist philosopher, 'You lament the expiring idea of home. It would not be expiring were it worth retaining. The domestic principle has fulfilled its purpose. The irresistible law of progress demands that another should be developed. It will come: you may advance or retard, but you cannot prevent it. It will work out like the development of organic nature. In the present state of civilization, and with the scientific means of happiness at our command, the notion of home should be obsolete. Home is a barbarous idea; the method of a rude age; home is isolation, therefore anti-social. What we want is community!' God grant there may be many a Gerard to answer 'It is all very fine; but I like stretching my feet on my hearth.'[9] Bravely and nobly said, true-hearted Saxon peasant; but – where are the coals?

Dukes and earls and Scotch political economists may theorize as they please, but until the people are rendered less dependent on that wealth, which seems perfectly well disposed to let them starve, and more dependent on their own exertions, and the bounty of Providence, to which they are still happily disposed to trust, Chartism and Strikes, Socialism and Incendiary Fires will continue to be the handmaid furies of English civilization.

In *Coningsby*, the intolerable servitude of the sovereign was described and deplored, and the people were taught to look for succour not to either of the political factions which for so long have enthralled the king, and cared not for them, but 'To fly from petty tyrants to the throne.' In *Sybil*, the grand opportunity which was offered in 1839 to Sir Robert Peel of vindicating the long lost prerogatives of the Sovereign, is maturely discussed . . . .[10] [8]

But a 'free monarchy' demands a free church, and if England suffers for want of the former, the absence of the latter is even a still greater and more severely felt evil. The mighty struggle in the seventeenth century was between the assertors of a free monarchy and a free church on the one side, and those who would enslave them, and by consequence the people, on the other. Strafford promised his royal master to make him the greatest king in Christendom, and employed all his marvellous energy and talent to raise the Irish church out of the miserable subserviency to the oligarchs in which he found her. Laud, while vindicating the highest monarchical prerogatives for Charles, placed the pontifical on an equality with the regale.[11] They were defeated; the Restoration produced a compromise, the Revolution a retrogression, and the altar and the crown are now equally depressed. The movement which elevates the one, will raise the other also. That the cause of the church is the cause of the people, is so plain that to announce it is but to state a truism. The church's material fabric is the poor man's richest and fairest palace; all other worldly glory is not for him; the [9] costly hangings, the gold, the glitter, the wines and dainty viands of the sons of wealth – in all these he has no part; but in the gorgeous windows, the embossed roofs, the thrilling anthems, and, above all, in the most sweet and awful altar-feast – in all these he claims his equal share: and woe to the State which hinders him in the enjoyment of those privileges! State patronage, and minister-made bishops, and impropriate tithes, and pews and pulpits – these have deprived the poor man of his rights, and the poor man's church of its most glorious characteristic.[12] Well may Mr. Milnes exclaim, after describing the effects produced by a London church,

> Who shall remove this evil
> That desecrates the age –
> A scandal great as ever
> Iconoclastic rage?
> Who this Christian people
> Restore their heritage?[13]

If Chartism had led its followers to do nothing worse than vindicate their right to Norwich Cathedral and the parish churches of England, we should become advocates of the charter. Mr. Disraeli seems to us to understand the true position which the clergy should adopt; and though Mr. St. Lys is an imperfect portrait of a Hook or a Manning, still he represents the great truth announced in *Coningsby*, that 'the priests of God are the tribunes of the people!'[14] And this it is, after all, which has given a power to the church movement of late years: if the people have not been on its side, it has been on theirs; and let ministers make what bishops they like, and middle-class plutocrats persecute whom they choose, that system and those men round whom are entwined the affections and sympathies of the poor will ultimately prevail.

We have thus briefly placed before our readers the main principles which are developed in *Sybil*: those principles are ours, for they are derived from Christ-Church and from King's. Let the youth of either University say whether those principles find a response in their hearts, or not. If we understand anything of the spirit that now is animating the 'true treasure of England,' the answer will be 'ay.' When the petty intrigues, and personal ambition, and mean imputations, which seem to be, not the deplorable though necessary accessories to, but the very staple of this decade's politics, shall be buried in oblivion, the historian of these times will relate that contemporaneous with the great religious movement which, commencing at Oxford and Cambridge, gave back vitality and energy to an enfeebled, erastianized Church, and ultimately unity to Christendom, there arose within the walls of St. Stephen's a voice which appealed to the Past and anticipated the Future, which denounced the [10] tawdry counterfeits that a spurious liberalism and an emasculated Conservatism had imposed upon a toiling population for ancient rights and English privileges, and upheld against the derision of routine politicians, the duties of the Rich and the nobility of the Poor! [11]

(ii)   The Spirit of the New Generation

Benjamin Disraeli, 'Preface', *Lothair*[15]

. . . [T]he general spirit of . . . [the Young England trilogy] ran counter to the views which had long been prevalent in England, and which may be popularly, though not altogether accurately, described as utilitarian. They recognised imagination in the government of nations as a quality not less important than reason. They trusted much to popular sentiment, which rested on an heroic tradition and was sustained by the high spirit of a free aristocracy. Their economic principles were not unsound, but they looked upon the health and knowledge of the multitude as not the least precious part of the wealth of nations. In asserting the doctrine of race, they were entirely opposed to the equality of man, and similar abstract dogmas, which have destroyed ancient society without creating a satisfactory substitute. Resting on popular sympathies and popular privileges, they held that no society could be durable unless it was built upon principles of loyalty and religious reverence. . . . [**xv**]

3 Extra-Parliamentary Perspectives

The importance ascribed to 'social reform' by members of the Young England Party in Parliament was endorsed by its supporters outside of Parliament. For the latter, however, it was explicitly linked to a more general quest for national regeneration and was made the basis of an appeal for the creation of a truly national movement.

(i) The Problem of Modern Society

[Anon.], 'A Young England Manifesto'[16]

A hundred years have elapsed since England witnessed a civil war; the strife of parties has ever since been waged in the press instead of the field; the sword has yielded to the pen, and the newspaper broadsheet has taken the place of the hostile banner. During this century of internal tranquillity, new interests has arisen, new elements of social life have been developed, and agencies of tremendous power have been at work changing the external framework of society, and dislocating all the joints and bands of its ancient constitution. . . . Such physical changes must have wrought great convulsions in the social system, and must work out still greater innovations, requiring to be watched by the wisdom of the philosopher as well as the prudence of the statesman; we have accumulated heavy responsibilities for the next generation; those youths who are about to enter the busy stage of life have to meet a state of society for which History affords no precedent, and experience furnishes no guidance.

Young England has little to learn from Old England; for during the past century of change Old England has done little more than adjourn perplexing questions . . . to a more convenient season, and has bequeathed its accumulation of social difficulties to be settled like the national debt, by an overburdened posterity. . . . Young England receives an inheritance of doubts, difficulties, and perplexities, all of which affect the ability of the empire and our social life as a people.

In this, the most wealthy empire on which the sun ever shone, and on whose dominions it never sets, . . . in this land, so richly endowed, and so highly favoured, there are thousands who are perishing for lack of food. The cry of famine mingles with the laugh of luxury; the shriek of misery is heard loud and high over the merriment of ease and comfort. Within view of the lordly hall, for the decoration of which Nature has lavished her treasures, and Art exhausted her resources, rises the hovel of the pinched and shivering peasant, with his dilapidated roof, broken windows, cold hearth, and empty table. . . .

But dreadful as is this physical destitution, the moral degradation which is its necessary consequence is still more fearful. Crime has ever been the constant concomitant of famine . . . .

Such fearful evidences of depravity, arising from destitution, show that the condition of the agricultural labourers cannot be neglected with impunity; and if Old England shrinks from the investigation, YOUNG ENGLAND must perforce gird itself to the task of inquiry.

The condition of the manufacturing population must not escape attention; the alternations of prosperity and depression to which our staple branches of industry are subjected, have acquired a periodicity which makes the recurrence of distress at definite intervals almost a matter of certainty. We have witnessed recently a commercial crisis, which threatened absolute ruin to the most populous districts of England. It is true that the danger is passed for the present, that the mills are in full work, the operatives employed, and the rate of wages considerably increased. Old England may congratulate itself on escape from dangers passed; but YOUNG ENGLAND has a future before it, and must therefore examine those principles of the commercial system which involve seasons of depression in their cycle. We must inquire whether there may not be limits within which it is the duty of the ruling powers to restrain speculation, and whether there may not be arbitrary restraints imposed upon some social elements which, if enfranchised, would ensure continuous progress. . . . [8]

[Anon.], 'The Principles of Young England'[17]

The sobriquet YOUNG ENGLAND has been sometimes applied in a tone of derision. White waistcoats and certain impracticable fancies have seemed to the superficial observer the characteristics of a new and rising body. We, however, assume the title in all earnestness, and in its proper signification. It is the Young Manhood of the British Nation – the experiment of the thoughts and principles upon which we believe the future destinies of our country depend. . . .

[D]uring the last thirty or forty years . . . the trading spirit has . . . become intensified beyond all precedent; the benefits which it scattered profusely in its progress concealed the seeds of evil which were being sown on all sides, from the absence of the proper counter-weights to its selfish tendencies. . . .

There had, however, been an under-current of feeling and thought gradually swelling into a torrent. . . . It was asserted, that the power of wealth, like all other power, required restraint; that obedience to the truths of political economy might most increase the wealth of the nation, but that its happiness depended upon obedience [9] to other truths; that cash payment did not supersede the duty to our neighbour; that fellow-creatures were not – could not be treated as machines; that it was most hazardous to bring men nominally free down to the condition of slaves; that if individuals forgot their duties, the Legislature was bound to interfere, to protect the employed from the employers; that *laissez-aller* could not be the motto of a Christian government; that the physical improvements of the poor could not be overlooked in any schemes of the philanthropist and patriot; that even the poorest must be thought of, spoken to, and legislated for, with the clear recollection that they possessed feelings, minds, and souls, like our own, and like ourselves, destined for immortality; that if our sense of duty did not rouse us to action, our danger should do so; that, in fact, the social condition of the British nation was such as to make statesmen and philosophers tremble for our existence as an honourable, high-minded, powerful, free, and Christian nation. . . .

YOUNG ENGLAND, then, flinging back ridicule in the face of the scorner, confidently appeals to every right-thinking man, and believes that there do exist a sufficient number who will cast aside the trammels of party, and, looking only at the goodness of intention, the awful importance of the subject, will cheerfully lose sight of minor differences, in the one conviction that the 'Social Condition of the British Empire' must be improved, unless the British name is to cease from among nations.

It is the cause of self-preservation, – the cause of duty, – the cause of civilization, – and, above all, the cause of morality and Christianity.[10]

(ii)   *A Plea for National Organization*

A Young Englishman, 'Letter to Benjamin Disraeli', 9 October 1844[18]

Few among the rising generation will contemplate the proceedings at . . . Manchester, without feeling their hearts warmed and elevated, with the consciousness that a benevolent change is stealing over the harsh utilitarianism of the past. The spirit of the past generation addressed itself blankly to the head; that of the present would . . . reform the head through the medium of the heart. The one was the spirit of Calculation – let us hope the other is the spirit of Humanity.

It is a great fact, that there *does* exist such simultaneous though yet undeveloped movement in the young minds of this country, a movement hostile to partisanship, and to religious sectarianism; hostile to all that would reduce man to a machine; and friendly to all that reaches the heart, to all that tends to fraternise mankind, by appealing to the bold sympathies of our race. – But, Sir, this mind-movement wants direction; it must be acted upon by the master spirits of the age. We of the provinces, rejoice to see so many of our young authors identify themselves with this movement; we rejoice to see genius in the van of humanity; and we kindle with the manly sentiments that vivify their predictions; but we also deplore the want of union, and of concerted effort. We hear of different isolated facts, illustrative of the tendency of the age; of a speech here, a new book there; but we hear nothing of com- bination, nothing of settled unity of purpose. We look for settled exposition of a settled political creed. We are anxious for the establishment of some literary organ, which shall concentrate scattered efforts, command attention by its ability and gain converts by the truthfulness of its representations. . . .

Now, Sir, the vast mass of discontent and subordination, the existence of which in the hearts of the people, is vouched for by the Chartism of the last few years, by the Welsh riots, and by the incendarianism of the Eastern counties;[19] the presence of unspeakable poverty in the houses of the mechanic and the peasant; the impotence of the national church, and the virulence of sectarianism; the decadence of a proper sympathy between the great classes of our community, between the employees and the employed, the peer and the peasant, the master and the man – said I, the decadence of proper sympathy, – say rather the active existence of mutual abhorrence – dread on the one part, sullen looks on the other; these, Sir, are all *results*, these are the *materials* which have furnished the *disposition* for a great social and political regeneration.

We have slept in a slumbering volcano; the elements of a fearful eruption are smouldering beneath us – we dread its culmination – let us hasten that it may be averted. Thus, conscious of social suffering, anxious for its amelioration, and fearful of its result, we have a disposition for regeneration – it is ascertained by the reflective, and unconsciously anticipated by even the thoughtless. The demonstration over which you recently so ably presided is one of its many exponents.

Now for the conduct which is to turn it to useful account. We look to you, Sir, as the man who first gave utterance to the mind-movement of the growing age. We look to you, and to your associates, to take advantage of that Disposition that you have ascertained. Let there be a plan of operation concerted; let there be an organ established for the dissemination of your views, let there be a society formed, to form a recognised nucleus round which isolated efforts may arrange themselves, and which should direct the now objectless aspirations of the new generation, and a host will be found to shoulder the work; and the blessing of Heaven be wanting to carry it to consummation.

Notes to Part I

1. Manners 1841.
2. Smythe 1844.
3. [Anon.] 1845a. This essay was a friendly notice of Disraeli's *Sybil* in *The Oxford and Cambridge Review*, a publication with close links to Young England. Many of the themes echo positions advanced by Manners (particularly the stress upon the role of the Church) but the treatment is leavened by touches that are reminiscent of Smythe's writings. It is possible that the article was a joint production.
4. Leading Young England figures were schoolboys at Eton and undergraduates at Cambridge; their mentor, Revd F. Faber, was a fellow of University College, Oxford. Members of the group gave widely reported speeches to audiences at Birmingham and Manchester (see pp. 133–7).
5. Anthony Ashley Cooper, Lord Ashley, later seventh Earl of Shaftesbury (1801–85), was a leading parliamentary figure in the campaign for factory legislation.
6. That is, Sir James Graham (1792–1861), Home Secretary in Peel's administration.
7. Hallam 1827, I, p. 85.
8. Thomas Carlyle's *Past and Present* appeared to great critical acclaim in 1843. William Sewell (1804–74), Fellow of Merton College, Oxford, and White's Professor of Moral Philosophy in the University, resisted Roman Catholic tendencies in the Tractarian Movement; the works referred to are: *Hawkstone; a tale of and for England in 184—* (1845) and 'Principles of Gothic Architecture' (1841).
9. Disraeli 1845, Bk III, ch. 9.
10. Disraeli 1844, Bk VII, ch. 2; Disraeli 1845, Bk IV, ch. 14.
11. As Lord Deputy of Ireland, the Earl of Strafford (1593–1641) compelled members of the nobility to restore property that had been embezzled from the Church. Archbishop William Laud (1573–1645) was an icon for High Tories in the early nineteenth century, but was vilified by those who took a sympathetic view of seventeenth-century challenges to royal and ecclesiastical authority.
12. Cf. Manners' speeches on Mortmain and National Holy-Days, below pp. 68–76, 88–93.
13. 'London Churches', (Milnes 1844b, p. 192).
14. Disraeli 1844, Bk VII, ch. 2. Walter Farquhar Hook (1798–1875) was Dean of Chichester from 1859. As Vicar of Leeds from 1837 Hook built new churches, schools and parsonage houses to meet the needs of a parish whose population had expanded rapidly as Leeds developed into a major commercial and industrial centre.

Henry Edward Manning (1808–92) was a leading supporter of Anglo-Catholic principles in the 1840s; he joined the Roman Catholic Church in 1851.

15. Disraeli 1870.
16. Young England (1845) 1 (4 January). Title supplied by the editor.
17. Ibid.
18. Hughenden Mss, 15/2/fos 135–6. This letter was written shortly after the widely publicized opening of the Manchester Athenaeum Institute by members of Young England; see below, pp. 133–7.
19. These signs of social dislocation were a common reference point in Young England statements; see below, pp. 73, 74, 82.

PART II

Young England on 'The Condition of England Question'

The documents printed in this section illustrate Young England views on what Thomas Carlyle called 'the Condition of England question', that is, the widespread debate in the 1830s and 1840s on the impact of rapid industrialization and urbanization on the condition of the working classes.[1] On one level, this debate focused on perceptions of growing impoverishment, unnecessarily harsh working conditions, uncertain employment, the effects of urban overcrowding, and growing signs of insubordination and unrest. At a more fundamental level, the debate raised questions about moral and spiritual dislocation and the erosion of values that were seen as being central to Christian conceptions of human and social well-being.

1 The Roots of the Problem

Although Young England was not dismissive of industrialization, its members believed that this process had been accompanied by radical shifts in social values and modes of social organization that dehumanized the working classes and undercut the basis of productive social interaction. This theme was expressed most forcefully in a speech made by William Busfield Ferrand to the House of Commons. Ferrand's attack focused upon the harmful effects of an ethos of unregulated competition upon the moral, material and social condition of workers in industrial areas. It concluded with a plea that government must reassume the protective role it had played before the onset of industrialization.

(i) The Commercial Spirit

William Busfield Ferrand, Notice of an Amendment to a Motion for the Repeal of the Corn Laws, House of Commons, 9 February 1843[2]

. . . [T]his House is of the opinion that the total repeal of the Corn-laws, instead of diminishing the present depression of trade, and the dreadful sufferings of the working classes, would tend greatly to increase the shock lately given to all those whose modes of thinking, feeling, and business have been regulated by living under a wise and benignant constitution, which has till lately, recognised the rights of property, the protection of industry, and the just and equitable requital of labour; under which great and extensive interests have grown up both in the agricultural, commercial,

47

William Busfield Ferrand

(*From the Alexander Turnbull Library, National Library of New Zealand,
Te Puna Mātauranga o Aotearoa*, ref no. S-L 196.)

and manufacturing property of the country; and that the preposterous conception of the present depression in trade being caused by the Corn Laws cannot have a place anywhere, except possibly in the minds of a few among our countrymen, hard pressed by the recent complications of commercial disaster, and predisposed accordingly to the most doleful imaginations, or of discarded ministers and greedy expectants of office. That a gambling principle has of late years entered into trade . . .; aided by the wholesale 'immigration' of labourers from the southern counties into the manufacturing districts, through the agency and at the express request of some of the Lancashire millowners, . . .; and that this gambling system has widely extended the sharp and rapidly increasing sufferings of all classes in the manufacturing districts, enlarged by the breadth of the changes effected in our agricultural and commercial system under the new tariff.[3] That the system lately introduced by many of the manufacturers in this country, of never recognising the principle that trade can only be healthy and prosperous when the supply keeps pace with the demand, has had a fatally paralysing influence upon all descriptions of trade, whilst the introduction of the power-loom, and the combing-machine have crippled to an astounding degree the industry of the manufacturing operatives, placed their labour at the mercy of their masters, and inflicted the most horrible sufferings on our high-hearted labouring population, by forcing that competition among them for employment, which is already keen and restless, altogether ruinous and destructive. That the sudden and splendid opulence lately acquired by many of the manufacturers of this country has been obtained by denying to labour its just requital, by grinding down the operatives into the dust for the purpose of 'equalising wages,' by the swindling truck system, and by destroying manual labour with the introduction of steam machinery, which has rendered reckless so many labourers, that heretofore had never quailed under misfortunes, nor ceased for a moment to place their trusts, so far as regarded human means, in their own dauntless spirit, their skilful fingers, and their indefatigable arms. That the period, foretold by the late Sir Robert Peel has at length arrived,[4] when the indiscriminate and unlimited employment of the poor has been, and is attended with effects so serious and alarming, that they cannot be contemplated without dismay; that the machinery of our manufactures has been brought to such perfection, that instead of being a blessing to the nation, it has been converted into the bitterest curse; and that as Parliament is omnipotent to protect, so is it bound under the most sacred obligations to deliver the poor out of the hands of their oppressors.

(ii)   The Erosion of Traditional Authority

In common with many of their contemporaries, Young England writers traced the ills of the present age to an erosion of social and political authority that occurred in the seventeenth and eighteenth centuries. But while progressive writers such as Thomas Carlyle embarked on a search for new forms of authority,[5] Young England cast nostalgic glances back to the dual system of clerical and monarchical authority which it associated with medieval, and with some periods of early-modern, history. Of all Young England writers Lord John Manners expressed the most unqualified regard for these aspects of the past.

Lord John Manners, 'Signs of the Times'[6]

> Methinks an earnest-minded man may see,
> In these our days of restlessness and strife,
> Portents with which our English air was rife
> What time religion and philosophy
> Cut off a sainted monarch's blameless life.
> The sick and fierce affection to be free
> From all restraints of Church and monarchy;
> The haughty confidence of power, that springs
> From out dull years of cold indifference,
> And weighs and counts the cost of holiest things,
> Asking the use of prelates and of kings,
> And views high mysteries with eye of sense, –
> Warn us that England once again may hear
> The shouts of Roundhead and of Cavalier. [89]

(iii)   The Legacy of the 'Glorious Revolution'

Young England statements of devotion to the past were accompanied by critiques of the oligarchic system that had dominated church and state since the 'Glorious Revolution' of 1688/9. During this period a corrupt remnant of the old nobility combined with financial adventurers and camp-followers of William III to produce a new social and political power block. Those who adhered to an authentically aristocratic ethos were marginalized, and the monarch was reduced to a position akin to that of a Venetian Doge. The new elite made the Church into an agency of a selfishly administered state and took advantage of the chill tones of Calvinistic Protestantism imported from Holland to establish an ecclesiastical, political and social system that was incompatible with Christian values and hostile to ideas of paternal monarchy and aristocracy.

Lord John Manners, 'William of Nassau'[7]

'Calm as an under-current,' that beneath
The green and slimy waters of some dyke
In chill, dank Holland glides (oh! how unlike
A sparkling English river, whose pure breath
Sends health and gladness over vale and heath,)
Came cold Dutch William, half afraid to strike
An open blow, in patricidal strife,
Against the gentle father of his wife;
So with insinuations worse than death
He worked upon credulity, and dared,
By filial love and piety unscared,
The mighty lie, wherewith base tongues were rife,
Against thy royal truth and spotless fame,
Thou gentlest bearer of the Virgin's name! [**94**]

[Note to this poem]

. . . I confess that, to my mind, there are in English history few more uninviting characters than William of Nassau; cold, calculating, regardless of the means by which his end was to be accomplished, devoid of natural affection, and unmoved by those generous sentiments which used to be regarded among Englishmen, – he has yet [**107**] been held up by the succeeding generations as a hero worthy to be worshipped; and the 'glorious, pious, and immortal memory' has been frantically honoured by men who would scorn themselves, were they to have made use of the means, for however worthy a purpose, by which he gained his crown. . . . I am glad to think, for the sake of English honour, that we are beginning to set up worthier idols in our hearts than this

Dutch conqueror, whom political rancour and religious intolerance combined to dignify as a patriotic deliverer. [**108**]

Benjamin Disraeli, *Sybil*[8]

If it be a salutary principle in the investigation of historical transactions to be careful in discriminating the cause from the pretext, there is scarcely any instance in which the application of this principle is more fertile in results, than in that of the Dutch invasion of 1688. The real cause of this invasion was financial. The Prince of Orange had found that the resources of Holland, however considerable, were inadequate to sustain him in his internecine rivalry with the great sovereign of France. In an authentic conversation which has descended to us, held by William at the Hague with one of the prime abettors of the invasion, the prince did not disguise his motives; he said, 'nothing but such a constitution as you have in England can have the credit that is necessary to raise such sums as a great war requires.' The prince came, and used our constitution for his purpose: he introduced in to England the system of Dutch finance. The principle of that system was to mortgage industry in order to protect property: abstractedly, nothing can be conceived more unjust; its practice in England has been equally injurious. In Holland, with a small population engaged in the same pursuits, in fact a nation of bankers, the system was adapted to the circumstances which had created it. All shared in the present spoils, and therefore could endure the future burden. And so to this day Holland is sustained, almost solely sustained, by the vast capital thus created which still lingers amongst its dykes. But applied to a country in which the circumstances were entirely different; to a considerable and a rapidly growing population; where there was a numerous peasantry, a trading middle class struggling into existence; the system of Dutch finance, pursued more or less for nearly a century and a half, has ended in the degradation of a fettered and burthened multitude. Nor have the demoralising consequences of the funding system on the more favoured classes been less decided. It has made debt a national habit; it has made credit the ruling power, not the exceptional auxiliary, of all transactions; has introduced a loose, inexact, haphazard, and dishonest spirit in the conduct of both public and private life; a spirit dazzling and yet dastardly; reckless of consequences and yet shrinking from responsibility. And in the end, it has so overstimulated the energies of the population to maintain the material engagements of the state, and of society at large, that the moral condition of the people has been entirely lost sight of.

A mortgaged aristocracy, a gambling foreign commerce, a home trade founded on a morbid competition, and a degraded people; these are great evils, but ought perhaps cheerfully to be encountered for the greater blessings of civil and religious liberty. Yet the first would seem in some degree to depend upon our Saxon mode of trial by our peers, upon the stipulations of the great Norman charters, upon the practice and the statute of Habeas Corpus, – a principle native to our common law, but established by the Stuarts; nor in a careful perusal of the Bill of Rights, or in an impartial scrutiny of the subsequent legislation of those times, though some diminution of our political franchises must be confessed, is it easy to discover any increase of our civil privileges. To those indeed who believe that the English nation, – at all times a religious and Catholic people, but who even in the days of the Plantagenets were anti-papal, – were in any danger of again falling under the yoke of the Pope of Rome in the reign of James the Second, religious liberty was per-haps acceptable, though it took the shape of a discipline which at once anathematized a great portion of the nation, and virtually establishing Puritanism in Ireland, laid the foundation of those mischiefs which are now endangering the empire. . . .

If James the Second had really attempted to re-establish Popery in this country, the English people, who had no hand in his overthrow, would doubtless soon have stirred and secured their 'Catholic and Apostolic church,' independent of any foreign dictation; the church to which they still regularly profess their adherence; and being a practical people, it is possible that they might have achieved their object and yet retained their native princes; under which circumstances we might have been saved from the triple blessings of Venetian politics, Dutch finance, and French wars . . . .

2 The Evils of the 'New' Poor Law

(i) The Inhumanity of the Poor Law System

In common with other contemporary proponents of social and political paternalism, and some radical thinkers, members of the Young England movement regarded the system of poor relief established by the Poor Law Amendment Act of 1834 as both a cause and a symptom of moral confusion and social derangement. Consequently, criticism of the 'new' Poor Law played an important role in statements of Young England principles both in Parliament and out-of-doors.

[Anon.] 'The New Poor Law'[9]

. . . Our readers may depend upon it, that there is something essentially wrong in the system that has excited and cherished in the hearts of the poor, in the rural districts, feelings of detestation so strong as those evinced against the workhouse system. . . . The avowed object of the framers of the new Poor Law was to *force* the poor to work, without consideration whether they could obtain work or not, and to inspire the labouring classes with 'a salutary dread' of the workhouse . . . . Poverty was treated as something approaching to a crime; and the applicant for parochial assistance was dealt with as a delinquent. The grand dogma of the Poor-Law Commission was one from which the soul shrinks with abhorrence, and which at once created in the hearts of the poor feelings of indignation and horror. . . . [26]

(ii)   An Unqualified Critique

William Busfield Ferrand, Speech on the Poor Law, House of Commons, 28 September 1841[10]

... Sir, in expressing my opinion of the New Poor Law, I declare it to be unconstitutional in the highest degree; it deprives the poor of the adequate relief, and protection to which they are entitled by the constitution of the country; it has, to a great extent, dried up the sources of charity. ... [5]

[...] Sir, I can identify the New Poor Law with the present disgraceful factory system. It was introduced in the north, on account of the factory labourers in Lancashire and Yorkshire being so reduced by death and disease, that the cotton-spinners found it impossible to carry on their rapidly increasing establishments with the number of hands that remained; they therefore entered into a deep-laid plot with the assistant Poor Law commissioners, and afterwards with the Poor Law Commissioners themselves. ... Sir, when the hon. Member for Manchester, (Mr. M. Phillips,) at the commencement of the session, moved the address in reply to the speech from the throne, he described, in language which must have sunk deep into the breast of every man of feeling who heard it, the dreadful state of misery and distress, nay, of absolute starvation, to which one hundred and two families in Manchester were reduced, for they had even to pawn their day-clothes to obtain covering for the night. ... Sir, that hon. Member recalled to my recollection the history of the rich man, who was clothed in purple and fine linen, [laugher from the opposition,] who possessed this world's goods, and who fared sumptuously every day, but refused to the poor man the crumbs which fell from his table.[11] ... Sir, that hon. member having these objects of distress daily before his eyes, afforded them no relief, but calmly and patiently wrote down their different cases of distress on paper, buttoned up his pockets, and then came into this House, and deliberately charged the landed proprietors of England with being the cause of the destitution of these poor wretches! ... But let me ask those hon. Members opposite, who are these hundred and two wretched families? Why *your own worn-out, cast-off machinery!* Out of whose sinews you have extracted your wealth, and then flung them away to die in misery and want. [Hear, hear.]

Sir, I remember that about two years ago a public dinner was given in Manchester by the anti-corn league cotton-spinners, at which they boasted they could buy up the landed property of the nobility of England; and, by way of adding éclat and effect, they asked over to it the hon. Member for Cork (Mr. O'Connell), who there asserted that 'the landlords' venison was sweetened with the widow's tears, and their claret dyed with the orphan's blood.'[12] . . . That language was cheered by the assembled cotton-spinners, but it was received with ineffable disgust by the working classes; so much so, that the hon. Member is now glad to pass [7] [un]noticed through that town. Had he been present tonight, I would have told him that his assertion was a foul calumny on the landlords; that such aspersions as he imputed to them, were 'alien to their blood, their country, and their religion.' [Loud cheers.]

In the sister kingdom of Ireland, the landed proprietors had been told by a subordinate government officer, that *'property had its duties as well as its rights;'*[13] and I also tell those boasting cotton-spinners that their immense wealth has *its* duties, as well as its rights, and that it is their bounden duty, instead of constantly *preaching* of the misfortunes and distresses of the poor, to *disgorge* some part of the enormous fortunes they have amassed out of their labour and sinews, and to relieve their present distresses. [Hear, hear, hear.] How different was their conduct from that of the landed nobleman! I tell the hon. Member [Mr Cobden[14]] that every farthing he has obtained by the cotton trade is sprinkled with the blood of the poor infant factory children. [Oh, oh, from the Opposition.] These manufacturers, by working their labourers *both day and night,* (for their avarice, like their toiling slaves, knows no rest,) have so glutted the markets, both at home and abroad, that they find it impossible to sell their goods, and although they have accumulated fortunes in a few years that would have amply repaid a long life of industry, they would unhesitatingly ruin the whole landed interest of England, to enable them to add it to their already overgrown wealth. . . .

Sir, I am convinced that food is sufficiently cheap in this country, if the operatives received a *'just requital'* for their labour; and I tell the manufacturers who come here to lay the blame of the misery *they* have caused upon the shoulders of the landed proprietors, that they themselves are the most avaricious and selfish class of all the holders of property. The landlords are very well content if their rents pay them three and a half per cent., but I doubt if these mill-owners are satisfied with a profit of one thousand per cent. [Oh, oh, and laughter, from the Opposition.] Sir, if I don't speak within bounds, what did they mean by boasting at the Manchester dinner that they could buy up the nobility of England? . . .

But I ask, is the misery, which is now *for the first time* so eagerly pressed upon our attention by hon. Gentlemen who are *now* on the Opposition side of the House, a phenomenon of yesterday? Has it never been known to exist in the manufacturing districts previous to the present year? . . . Sir, I ask hon. Gentlemen opposite, if the Corn Laws produced this dreadful state of destitution and distress, when their cotton trade was in a most flourishing condition? . . . The hon. Member for Manchester (Mr. Gibson[15]) quoted, the other night, the opinions of a chaplain extraordinary, the Rev. Baptist Noel, to prove that the Corn Laws had produced all the existing distress. I, too, will quote to the House the opinions of a man, who, during a long life, has studied the whole subject of the causes which have produced the present distress of the working classes in the manufacturing districts, and who has laboured night and day in this good work: – his own approving conscience, his guide – a cell in the Fleet prison his reward. [Ironical cheers.] You (the Opposition) cry, Hear, hear, – you rejoice in this man's sufferings, – yes, you may imprison his body, but you *cannot* imprison his soul, for Mr. Oastler is even now engaged in forwarding the welfare of the operatives by his *Fleet Papers*, and in whose hearts and affections he *reigns* as triumphantly as ever. Yes, Sir, it was Richard Oastler who put a stop to the horrid system of dragging the poor people in the South of England out of their humble cottages, and driving them from their green fields and shady lanes, into the fetid atmosphere of a cotton-mill, and the dark, damp cellar of an alley in Manchester, that they might for a short time fill up the places of those who had been brought to a premature death by this accursed system, but soon to follow after in the ceaseless train [9] of its victims.[16] . . . Could the hon. Members opposite, who possessed mills, be aware of the dreadful misery which the factory system entailed upon their work-people? If they were, he did not believe there was a man living, who ought to be thought actuated by honourable principles, who could bring such charges against the landed proprietors as had been repeated in that House, when it was notorious throughout the manufacturing districts that they were not in the least to blame, for the distress which prevailed there was entirely owing to the overworked factory system, and the forgetfulness of the mill-owners, that '*property has its duties, as well as its rights.*' . . . . [11]

Sir, I proclaim here in the assembled Commons' House of England, that this country is a land of slavery. [Hear, hear! And No, no! from the opposition] I repeat the assertion, and defy contradiction, that *this is a land of slavery:* that the men, women, and children in the south have been regularly picked, bought, sold, and invoiced by the poor-law commissioners of England to the cotton-spinners in Lancashire; there to be worked to death. Can any man deny it, who has heard the details which I have this night read? If you [the opposition] do, I appeal to the people of England, and *they* shall be the judge.

Sir, the poor are now crying aloud for succour. I will therefore describe to the House what the right hon. Baronet, the member for Tamworth, recommends for the relief of those distressed wretches in Lancashire, whose miserable state has been brought before the notice of the House . . . . [13] . . . . Sir, in one of the debates in this house the right honourable baronet stated – 'I am one of those who have derived our fortunes from the industry of the operative classes, and I trust that others who owe their prosperity to the same cause will feel, as I do, that it is our duty to relieve the public, by taking on ourselves the charge of a just requital to those classes from whom our prosperity has sprung.'[17] Sir, I ask those hon. Members to follow this just and reasonable advice; for how can they reconcile their enormous wealth with the present dreadful distress which they state to exist among their own work people? And if any one of them can lay his head upon his pillow this night without feeling a deep conviction that he at least has done his *'duty'* to them, I envy him not his repose. . . .

(iii)   The Poor Law and Local Paternalism

George Smythe, Speech to Electors at Canterbury, 19 January 1841[18]

Where it [the Poor Law] is well administered, as in parts of Leicestershire, not in the spirit of Somerset House, but under the auspices of the Duke of Rutland,[19] it is productive of good. But where it operates tyrannically, and where it is converted into a monstrous abuse, it must necessarily be bad and require revision and modification.

Lord John Manners, Speech on the Poor Law in Ireland, House of Commons, 19 June 1843[20]

. . . Sir, it is impossible that any one who has paid the slightest attention to Ireland, not to feel persuaded that the Poor Law system as it is attempted to be carried out, is a most effective cause of discontent, and I earnestly hope the Government will cease from endeavouring to alter by such a change as the Poor Law necessitates, the old manners and ancient feelings of a generous-hearted **[114]** people; I implore them to desist from striving to effect such a revolution. I implore them on the contrary to do all that in them lies, by accepting their traditional habits and ideas, by appealing to and governing by their unhesitating faith, and hereditary feudalism, to render that which is at best a Legislative Union, a real and cordial Union of a loyal, prosperous, and contented people. **[115]**

3 Addressing the Condition of England Question

As well as criticizing contemporary values and practices, Young England writers promoted a number of measures which they thought would provide solutions to aspects of 'the Condition of England question'. Within Parliament Young England figures threw their weight behind proposals for allotment schemes and for regulating the working conditions in factories. Demands for state-supported systems of popular education were not given priority by Young Englanders in Parliament, but they formed an important plank in extra-parliamentary programmes. In addition to these responses, which were common to a number of contemporaries, members of Young England proposed ways of restoring the values and social relationships which they believed had been undermined in the course of recent history. Manners was the most active in these endeavours. He attempted to revive forms of popular culture that were integrated with systems of clerical and secular paternalism and oversight in order to reintroduce traditional values and relationships in a modern context. He also appealed for the establishment of monastic institutions in urban centres so that the Church could more effectively perform its pastoral role, and proposed changes in laws regulating the bequest of landed estates so as to make the Church reliant upon the charitable impulses of its members, rather than upon an unsympathetic state.

(i) *Allotments for the Working Classes*

William Busfield Ferrand, Speech on the Allotment of Waste Lands, House of Commons, 30 March 1843[21]

. . . The mortality and immorality of the population now crowded in the manufacturing [**184**] districts, were . . . frightful in the extreme. Was there no remedy to rescue this portion of the population from their misery? Were the functions of Parliament at an end, or were they able to redress the grievances of the people? They were told to look to foreign colonisation for a remedy. Were they to send abroad to die unpitied and unheard-of, the peaceable and loyal subjects of this country, who had a right to exist in the country where they were born? . . .

What he proposed to ask the House to do was to restore the poor again to their comforts, and he proposed to do this by an allotment to them of the waste lands. He asked for . . . [this] as an act of justice: he asked for it in the name of the law of England – a law acknowledged by the greatest writers on the law and the constitution of England for centuries. . . . **[185]**

In many parts of the country the working classes, more particularly the poorer portion of them – and he spoke positively with regard to many of the handloom weavers in his own neighbourhood – had been enabled to live comfortably through the enjoyment of these rights, which of late years had thus been taken away from them. If every hon. member in that House would declare his conscientious conviction after a due consideration of this subject, he would certainly avow himself to be in favour of the allotment system. . . . He was sure that he should convince the House that if the allotment system of waste lands were adopted, it would prove, to a great extent, the salvation of the country; for it must be clear to all, that if something were not done for the working classes, and that speedily, the consequences would be most serious. The Government were sitting on the verge of a volcano at the present moment, which might burst forth with mischievous effect, unless precaution-ary measures were taken. . . . **[187]**

[A]t a time when the working classes were so much distressed . . . there was . . . much difficulty in keeping the peace of the country . . . . He knew that any such disturbances could and would be put down by the strong arm of the law; but would it not be more gratifying to be able to say that they had done justice to the poor, by restoring to them their rights, and placing them beyond the reach of temptation and want, and making them once more happy, and contented, and peaceable subjects? . . . **[190]**

He begged the House to listen to his appeal in behalf of the poor man. Give the poor a small allotment of land and a spade to cultivate it, and it would have the effect of diminishing the number of inmates in the union workhouses. The poor man then would not be deprived of the privilege of attending at his usual place of worship. Give the poor, before they were weighed down to the dust, what they had a right to demand. He maintained it was the right of the poor – a right of which they had for centuries been plundered. **[197]**

Lord John Manners, Speech on the Allotment of Waste Lands, House of Commons, 21 June 1843[22]

It was all very well to say, the labourers should be dependent on wages only, but he did not think that any one who was acquainted with the manufacturing districts could expect that families could be wholly dependent on manufacturing wages. Two or three days a week they had labour. How could that make them independent? He had presented several petitions from the manufacturing classes of Leicestershire, stating their wish for the allotment system, in order to eke out a subsistence. . . . It was an honourable mode of doing it. He was prepared to maintain that there was nothing more ennobling than agricultural labour; and it was still more the case of the man who felt he was the cultivator of his own field. [**188**]

Lord John Manners, Speech on Field-Garden Allotments, Bingley, 11 October 1844[23]

. . . I believe . . . that this allotment system . . . will go far to rectify what I cannot help looking upon as a serious and a growing evil – I mean the extinction of every agricultural class between that of the rich tenant-farmer and that of the day-labourer. . . . I am not unaware of the advantages derived from the system [**36**] of large farms; all that I contend for is, that they should not swallow up all farms of smaller dimensions . . .; and I look to the allotment system, as I trust it will be hereafter developed, as (to a certain degree at any rate) a corrective of that melancholy state of things. I call it melancholy, because we all know that contentment must spring from hope; and because no one can pretend to say, where there are no holdings but large farms, that there the peasant can ever entertain a hope of rising out of that condition in which he has been placed. . . . I do not say that it ever was the custom, or that it ever will be the custom, for many of the peasantry of England to rise from their condition and become farmers; but this I do say, that the system must be wrong which denies the possibility of such a condition being realised; and again I say, I look to the allotment system for a correction of that abuse. . . . [**37**]

Richard Monckton Milnes

(*From the Alexander Turnbull Library, National Library of New Zealand, Te Puna Mātauranga o Aotearoa*, ref no. S-L 192.)

(ii) The Regulation of Working Conditions in Factories

Richard Monckton Milnes, Speech on the Ten Hours' Bill, House of Commons, 22 March 1844[24]

. . . He hoped he might be excused from speaking earnestly upon this subject, because he did feel that it was now almost impossible to meet this question with the same calmness that was becoming and most just on a previous occasion. The hon. Baronet the Member for the Tower Hamlets, who had just addressed the House, had indeed undertaken a most difficult task. While every other Member seemed to feel that the question was one of enormous difficulty – while it appeared to be the general opinion, that whether the remedy proposed was right or not, yet the evils were great and undoubted [**1397**] – while those evils were generally allowed and unchallenged, that hon. Baronet had undertaken the task of representing the whole matter as a mere dream of philanthropic enthusiasts, and of holding up the factory women and children of this country as persons in so happy and contented a position that it would be most impertinent for the Legislature to interfere with them. He had hoped that that part of the question had long since been settled. He thought that the House felt the enormity of the evils, and that a national guilt had been incurred by the miseries of the unrestricted factory system. They knew that by that system they were bringing up millions of their fellow-creatures in a state of degradation almost lower than that of any slave population. They knew that there were thousands of factory children who had no possible means of receiving either moral or religious instruction. They knew that thousands of them had perished on the very threshold of manhood, it being physically impossible for them, from their exhausted strength, to obtain by labour any of the comforts of life. . . . [**1398**]

Lord John Manners, Speech on the Ten Hours' Bill, House of Commons, 22 March 1844[25]

By that decision you told the toiling people of England that party difference or indifference to this question was at an end, and that the Legislature was prepared to interfere in behalf of labour . . . . [**1420**] By that decision, you caused joy and smiles to prevail wherein before, was nothing but despair – and yet that decision you now propose to reverse. You then held out to the parched lips of toil and neglect the cup of hope – will you now dash it to the ground untasted? I would entreat this House, I would implore this Committee, to reflect for a moment on what has occurred during the last three years. Have you learnt nothing from the manufacturing insurrection in the north – have you learnt nothing from the agrarian rebellion in Wales – nothing from the indifference with which your labourers in Cambridgeshire and elsewhere regard your flaming homesteads, and fired corn-ricks? Do all these things teach you nothing? Methinks, when the storm does arise, and the waves of anarchy begin to break upon the barriers of the Con-stitution, and when all you hold dear and value shall be swept away in the general desolation a poor consolation it will be to you to reflect that such a melancholy result has arisen from your refusal to interfere in behalf of the over-worked labourer who toils beyond human endurance at the manufactures of England, albeit that refusal may be in accordance with the strictest canons of political economy. **[1421]**

Richard Monckton Milnes, Speech on Hours of Labour in Factories, House of Commons, 13 May 1844[26]

. . . What was the distinction between the slave and the free man? In the case of the slave his time was his master's . . .; slavery might be said to consist in one man holding his life at the will of another. But what was life? It was the living hour. It was the power of receiving religious, intellectual, and moral improvement. This constituted the chief distinction between the freeman and the slave. The free labourer ought to be free in some other sense, than to be free to starve, or free to break the law if he chose to take the risk of punishment. It became the Legislature, then, to remove the evils which the factory system presented to the improvement of the freeman with as much zeal and earnestness as they had shown in removing slavery. . . . **[1022]**

Believing confidently . . . in the successful result of this measure, then or at some future period . . . he hailed this Bill as the harbinger of a better system of legislation than had hitherto prevailed. He hailed that fusion of party which they then witnessed as something better than the binding of hon. Members for the purpose of misrepresenting their opponents. . . . **[1027]**

(iii)   *Popular Education*

[Anon.], 'The Education of the Working Classes'[27]

We are inclined, for our part, to regard education as the root of all permanent improvement in the character and moral condition of the working classes, and we look forward, we trust with no Eutopian expectation, for days when normal schools, steam, and other agencies now at work shall effect a complete revolution in the state of the people.; – when, so to speak, the fountains of the sublime and the beautiful, in conception and sentiment, which the great geniuses of past times and our own supply, shall be equally open to all, – a public source of refinement and emulation. Nor is this an extravagant or enthusiastic view of the matter: there is perhaps more of the romantic and ideal tendencies in the poorest than in the middling classes of society; and perhaps more vivid appreciation of what is exalted in heroism, or touching in pathos, among them. Why, then, should so many sources of gratification be denied them? Let adequate means be afforded, and narrow-minded prejudices set aside, and we can readily perceive an epoch when the weary sons of toil, though their brows be damp, and their hands begrimed with honest labour, shall nevertheless feed the inner man with the lofty ideas and glowing ideas of their more intellectual brethren; when all classes shall mutually approve each other pursuits; when the mechanical and scientific, the speculative and the practical, shall mingle in friendly intercourse; when handiwork shall interchange its work-day thoughts with the dreamy reveries of the philosopher and the theorist; when all the orders and divisions into which a people are necessarily broken, as various in their capacities and pursuits as they are in physiognomy and character, shall, like the many-coloured fragments of the kaleidoscope, combine and harmonize in every different relation into which it is possible for them to be placed. . . . [**186**]

(iv)   The Revival of Popular Culture

Lord John Manners, Speech at the Birmingham Athenic Institution, August 1844[28]

. . . He would not detain them by reciting the various games and modes by which the spirits of the people were upheld, their physical energies brought fully into operation, and that delightful and necessary relaxation afforded which contributed to establishing their character for mirth, health, and cheerfulness. They were well known, but, [**5**] unhappily for the present generation, only known by name to the great mass of the population. Unfortunately those manly games were not now publicly provided for the people. Under what circumstances and encouragement, and by whose good aid and wishes, were the members of that institution enabled to take their part in those manly and useful sports? Why, it was owing simply and entirely to their own exertions – to their own peaceable, laudable, and energetic exertions – and not to any public provision which had been made for them; not to any efforts on the part of those whose duty he held it to be to provide for the wants of the industrious classes in that respect. . . . But there was another and still more important object connected with their institution, namely, that of uniting together again the different classes of society. It was his firm conviction, founded upon something like a careful examination of history, that in days long gone by, when the unhappy separation of classes which now existed in this country was not known in the land, there was far more peace, more real happiness, and more complete security for all classes, than had existed, or could exist under such a class system as now prevailed in society. ... He knew very well that it was deemed unphilosophical to revert to those days and times, and the ancient customs of their forefathers; but, believing as he did that in those ancient days the peer lost nothing by his condescension, and that the poor were great gainers by it, he saw no reason why they should not dwell with pleasure on those days, and why he should not, if he could, encourage and support any legal, just, and prudent [6] associations which would have the effect of restoring at least some portion of that fine feeling which existed amongst the people in bygone days, and which would elevate the character of those who ought to be considered the pride and glory of their country. [7]

Lord John Manners, Speech on Field-Garden Allotments, Bingley, 11 October 1844[29]

... [T]he opening of the Bingley Cricket Club ... is a subject on which I feel ... a great deal can be said, for the time was when kings of England did not think it beneath them to apply their talents and devote their time to regulate and encourage the manly sports and pastimes of their people. ... No man, however elevated, in those days, ever thought of an amusement selfish and apart from the peasants and artisans of his country. I will not mention the names of many of those pastimes; many of them have died out; but I may say that cricket ... is manly, bracing, and brings together in harmonious contact the various classes of society; and therefore I say you do right well to establish conjointly with the allotment system a cricket club. May the two ever flourish together .... The same system which had decreed the peasant should never rise out of the rank he was born in, also denied him any amusement but the alehouse – any rest but on a Sunday; what wonder, then, that the old landmarks were beginning to disappear, and a new and strange [38] antipathy to be seen between the employer and the employed? The estrangement, then, which unfortunately has undoubtedly taken place between the various classes of society, where your good example is followed, will give place to cordial sympathy, to the performance of duties and responsibilities on the part of the rich, and to contentment and loyalty on the part of their less fortunate fellow-countrymen. . . . [**39**]

Lord John Manners, *A Plea for National Holy-Days*[30]

> All manner of persons within the Church of England shall from
> henceforth celebrate and keep the Lord's Day, commonly
> called Sunday, and *other Holy-days* according to God's holy
> will and pleasure, and the orders of the Church of
> England prescribed in that behalf.

It has of late years been made frequently a source of complaint that the English people, who of yore were famous over all Europe for their love of manly sports and their sturdy good humour, have year after year been losing that cheerful character, and, contrariwise, been acquiring habits and thoughts of discontent and moroseness. It is true that, in towns, debating clubs, and reading rooms, and halls of science, and gin-shops have sprung up with a mushroom speed of growth: and many humane and good people imagine that a course of astronomy, or a lecture on geology, is all the recreation of mind or body that a man who works sixty hours a week requires.[31] I am strongly persuaded to the contrary, that, at the risk of being laughed at as a blind bigot, I am going to express as well as I can my views as to the desirableness of restoring NATIONAL HOLY-DAYS and RECREATIONS – not, perhaps, without a humble hope that those higher in authority will take the subject into their consideration, and produce some well defined scheme that shall effectually banish to oblivion these few straggling hints.

We have gained great triumphs in China and India,[32] [**3**] and have thus terminated two very wicked and cruel wars; and accordingly the guns have been fired, and the church bells have been rung, and the nation is to celebrate with a holy-day the advent of peace. This, of itself, is very cheering to all who love the good old ways of our forefathers, and may still further justify my little essay; but how will that holy-day be observed? What means for duly and happily celebrating it are at hand for the great masses of the people? In cathedral cities, for instance, will the poor, and the needy, and the friendless throng into those glorious buildings, which the piety of our ancestors raised for them, to bear their part in thanking the Lord of Hosts for his late mercies, and then on the common outside the walls, or in the square within, join in lawful recreations, such as 'dancing, either men or women, archery for men, leaping, vaulting, or any other such harmless recreations?'[33] – where the lusty apprentice shall not fear to outleap his master's son, nor the pauper's heir to contend with the guardian's brother, while the alms of the faithful that were collected at the offertory in the morning are making the widows' and the orphans' hearts sing with joy? Or in the rural village, again, will the old parish church send out of its time-honoured portals the old men and women, the lads and lasses, to the [4] merry green, where youth shall disport itself, and old age, well pleased, look on? Alas! no. Utilitarian selfishness has well nigh banished all such unproductive amusements from the land: has it not also banished contentment, and good humour, and loyalty from thousands of English cottage homes?

But it will be said that I am strangely perverting fact. I shall be told that there never was a period when amusements were so diversified or so refined: whole treatises have been written during the last ten years on every imaginable sport; every county in England possesses its pack of fox-hounds, or its harriers – shooting may be said to have reached the pitch of perfection; more game is probably slaughtered now-a-days on a first of September, with all imaginable ease, than was used to be killed with difficulty in a whole year under good Queen Bess; and our breed of race-horses is the admiration of the world. This is all very true: but, with a partial exception in favour of the latter, I must contend that these sports are the sports of the higher, and not of the lower orders: and that, conducive as I believe them to be to the formation of a manly, robust character among those who enjoy them, their very excellence so far from constituting an objection to a revival of humbler sports for the humbler classes, is the strongest argument in its favour. [5]

Many people, however, would at once admit, as a general principle, the advantage of holy-days and public diversions for the people, and praise the political far-sightedness of Greece, Rome, and Constantinople, whose lawgivers and emperors seem to have regarded the amusement of the people as much as those of modern England too often seem to do their own: it is only when they are requested to put their general principle into particular practice that they discover insuperable objection – some from a regard to the pecuniary interest of the people – some from a respect to the sober reserve of the national character. As these, undoubtedly, are the two objections which can with most force be urged, I will apply myself to them, in the hope of removing or diminishing their cogency.

And here I will not refrain from adding my humble protest against the national idolatry paid to wealth, to those which have of late so seasonably appeared from divines and philanthropists. The country is flooded with money [6] . . . [but where] countless temples of wealth and speculation are daily rising, hundreds and thousands of temples raised to God are lying in crumbling ruins; . . . the collective wisdom of that nation has straightly and sternly refused spiritual food for *six* millions of souls; that against rights, and prayers, and highest eloquence, it pared down to the meanest utility the funds wherewith 'holy men of old' had endowed existing cathedrals; that prisons and houses of correction are the only buildings it raises for the people; and that it would regard the man, who should venture [7] to propose a grant of public money for the temporal recreation or eternal welfare of its poor, as a madman or a bigot.

So long, perhaps, as such strange inconsistencies degrade our private mercantile adventures and our public legislative enactments – so long as the spirit and conduct of the age is at once so profuse and so niggard – generous, yet so sparing – so democratic, and yet so careless of the poor – so long it may be deemed a sufficient reply to any proposals for shortening the hours of factory labour, or reviving holy-days and sports among the people, to say, 'We are too poor; time is money, and we cannot afford it.' But I will fain hope that this fever-fit of mammon worship[34] is beginning to abate: many people of great goodness and learning doubt, and are venturing to express their doubt, whether the one great object of social government in this kingdom, commonly called 'Church and State,' is to squeeze the greatest possible amount of wealth out of the greatest possible amount of work; and here and there gardens have been planted, and museums built, and occasionally even a holy-day provided for the working classes and the poor; while, which to me is the most cheering sign of all, a holy crusade has been commenced, and is being carried on with no inconsiderable success, against pews and other obstructions to their Church rights.[35] [8]

Another very gratifying symptom of a return to a healthier feeling must not be overlooked, in the merchants on 'Change resuming earlier hours, and the bankers having determined to close their banks earlier in the day: all these are steps in the right direction, and forbid me to despair of seeing none but Eton boys duly enjoying the holy-days of the Church. This money argument, if good against such a revival, is also good against the few holy-days that are yet left, and indeed against all restrictions on work and gain; nor shall I be easily convinced, that if the relations between employer and employed are what they ought to be in a Christian country, and what they certainly once were in this, the observance of a score of holy-days during the year would press upon the latter's means of support. **[9]**

. . . I now approach the other main objection which is drawn, or rather supposed to be drawn, from the national character of England; people seem to reason thus: – 'The English labourer is the most industrious, hardworking, sober of his class in the world; he would not know what to do with a holy-day if **[10]** you gave him one; and, industrious and sober as he is while working six days a week, only look at him when something extraordinary occurs to give him a holy-day time – an election, a new king, or a coming of age: he makes a beast of himself, and that clearly shows that he is better without a holy-day than with one.'

Putting aside the shockingly low view of English nature, which people who think thus must entertain, I should argue from their own premises to a very different conclusion. If it is true that, at these occasional cessations from work, the English labourer breaks loose from propriety, is it not because he has been so long bound to one unvarying course of toil that he knows not rightly how to appreciate or use the unwonted holy-day? It would be as logical to argue against holy-days for school-boys, from their pea-shooting, and making faces at all the good folks they meet in their wild glee on their road home, as to conclude that because, as things now are, an election or a coronation produces a debauch, the fewer holy-days the people have, the better it is for their morals. Indeed, it is a strange contradiction to aver that the English labourer is so steady and plodding that he does not want a holy-day; and then, that when he has one, he loses all his steadiness, and runs riot in dissipation. The truth is, as in many other matters, the abuse springs from the non-use. **[11]** . . .

Perhaps nothing strikes an Englishman abroad more forcibly than the attention paid to the amusements of the people: and yet *attention* is not the proper word; the amusements seem to spring spontaneously from the spirit of the nation; nor do I think that climate or religion has as much to do with it as some suppose. In Catholic Biscay, or Protestant Pays de Vaud, the saint's-day and the *jour de fete* are alike a holy-day to the people.[36] I know no sight more pleasing, no sound more cheerful, than those presented by the plaza or paseo of the humblest Spanish town on the evening of a festival – the grave but happy people tripping it to pipe and tabor, while those of the higher orders saunter about, entering into the pleasures of the scene, and at hand by their presence and authority to check any incipient irregularity. How long shall we be content coldly to admire whatever is good in foreign countries, while we sedulously abuse and clumsily emulate their crimes and follies? **[12]** . . .

Nor is there . . . truth in the generally received idea of coldness and reserve stamping the English character. That a Saxon, or Norman-Englishman, is not as light as a Provencal Frenchman, or as gay as a Milesian, I readily acknowledge; but any one conversant with history, or who has lived in those parts of England – the lakes, for instance – where old customs and the old character still linger, must confess that the 'all work and no play' system, which is defended as adapted to the English character, and the modern and unchristian bars which now separate wealth from poverty, have their source elsewhere than in the English national character.

I will go still further, and say that, instead of 'English coldness,' 'Dutch phlegm' would be the appropriate term. Merry England continued to merit her epithet as long as the Stuarts [14] reigned over her; and it is a remarkable fact, that the first of the Hanoverian dynasty who identified himself with English feelings, King George the Good – he who said it was his wish that every Englishman should read his Bible – also wished to restore the sports and games to his people, of which Puritan bigotry and scornful latitudin-arianism had deprived them.[37] May we hope that it has been reserved for his fair and gentle successor to witness the accomplishment of both his noble wishes!

To show how dear to the people, even in the middle of the seventeenth century, their old holy-days and sports were, the Puritans, in the height of their triumphs, after they had destroyed Maypoles and abolished festivals, were forced to decree, by public ordinance, the second Tuesday in every month (I wonder they did not select Friday) sacred for the purpose of recreation. [15] . . .

At the Restoration, in many places, the reaction against Puritan gloom and tyranny brought back the old sports and holy-days, which here and there have survived even to this day. Mr. Bandinel, in the *Churchman* for October, 1842, says –

> At Shillingstone, a village situated between Blandford and Sturminster, in Dorsetshire, Mayday is kept with all due honour. There is a very fine Maypole there, and the good old customs are maintained in full force. The wreaths are hung up and left till they wither; and the injunctions of King Charles I. and Archbishop Laud are, in many points, scrupulously obeyed.[38]

At Ambleside, the custom of decorating the church once a year with flowers is still kept up, and any one who has spent a 'rushbearing Sunday' there, can hardly have failed to observe how deep a root has the old rite struck in the affection of the villagers.[39] But, indeed, every village in England has some memorial, however slight, left of the national feeling in favour of, not against, the [16] old holy-days; and I should think the very sight of Mr. Strutt's book on our 'Sports and Pastimes' would convince any one, that if they, and the days on which they were celebrated, have fallen, as they confessedly have, into desuetude, it is not because they were alien to the character of the English nation.[40]

 . . . Let me dwell a little on some of the benefits reasonably to be anticipated [from a revival of national holy-days]. And first and most important of them all would I rank the opportunity [17] thus given to the poor of duly honouring the Church's holy-days. How often do we hear the Church of England called, sometimes fondly, sometimes arrogantly, 'the poor man's Church;' but, alas! how sadly have secular influences, the carelessness of the State, the worship paid to wealth, diminished, of late years, the practical justice of her claim to that glorious title.[41] She, indeed, hath appointed divers services for thirty-six days in the year, but in how many of them are the poor permitted to join? Or do people really believe that these are the luxuries of religion intended for the rich and idle alone? When 'the curate,' after the Nicene Creed, 'declares unto the people what holy-days or fasting-days are in the week following to be observed,' is he speaking but to the wealthy among them? No one, I believe, would answer these questions in the affirmative; and yet modern practice would justify such an answer. In several rural parishes, where saints'-days services have been established, or revived, at hours most suited for the labouring population, a readiness has been shown to attend them;[42] and we have abundant reason to hope that, were the observance of them encouraged, rather than discouraged, by modern laws and habits, not only would our churches be filled with humble worshippers, but the poor and needy would feel, in many little and unsuspected ways, far more [18] than they can feel now, that the Church is indeed to them a mother – an endless well of comfort and consolation, running over with blessings, temporal and eternal, alike in the heats of Lammas or the snows of Christmas.

 And if such would be the gain to the religious happiness of the people – if the Churchman would rejoice at such a realization of their Church privileges, can the statesman detect in it no security for the constitution it is his aim to guard? Is a religious and a contented population more to be feared than one careless of eternity, ignorant of the past, and discontented with the present? . . . Let the history and the spread of Chartism and Socialism supply the answer. From year to year, as wealth has been accumulating and simplicity dying away –

as new habits have come in and the old ones gone out – as traditional holy-days have been disregarded and fresh hours and days of work obtained; so, in proportion, have dissent [19] and discontent, anarchy and infidelity advanced; until now, when scarce a Maypole is left in England, or a holy-day observed, the banks of the mighty river of spent-up sin and misery are beginning to give way, and men shrink from contemplating the impending deluge.

Nor is this the only danger to be apprehended from the monstrous system of 'all work and no play,' as it has been aptly called by the *Spectator*. Late medical and statistical reports give, unfortunately, abundant evidence that King James's wise foresight was not deceived when he said that

> this prohibition of holy-days and games barreth the common and meaner sort of people from using such exercises as may make their bodies more able for war, when we, or our successors, shall have occasion to use them; and in place thereof sets up filthy tipplings and drunkenness, and breeds a number of idle and discontented speeches in their alehouses. *For when shall the common people have leave to exercise, if not upon Sundayes and holy-dayes, seeing they must apply their labour and win their living in all working dayes?* . . .[43]

It is to be regretted that . . . the evil which the wisdom of the Stuarts guarded against is admitted and deplored, their simple and efficacious remedy is lost sight of . . . . [22] Now, though a good deal may undoubtedly be done to improve the air of Spitalfields, still I take it a more frequent inhalation of country breezes is what is really wanted; and how can that be obtained, save by an increase of rest days? And again, what days can so properly be selected as those mentioned by King James as 'holy-dayes' – the festivals of the Catholic Church in England? The promoters of the wretched Mortmain law of 1736, among other arguments of curious infelicity in its favour, alleged – and this allegation was mainly relied on – that, should any more land be tied up in Mortmain, great danger would arise to the country, in case of invasion, from the consequent decay of military skill and spirit in the nation.[44] I apprehend that, in a military and national point of view, we have more to fear from the physical and moral decay of the serfs of wealth, than from that of the tenants and dependants of the Church; and that if it be the duty of a paternal and religious Government, as I suppose most will admit it to be, to foster by all means the national strength, which is the national defence, and to ward off all that may impair it, it becomes now the duty of the Government to raise the depressed condition of the working classes, by returning to [23] the everlasting, because Christian – ever applicable, because Catholic, measures of our wise forefathers.

. . . I have thus endeavoured, after removing objections that might previously be urged against it, to touch upon, rather than develop, some of the advantages reasonably to be expected from a recurrence to the observance of holy-days; but I will not dismiss the subject without stating my sincere conviction, that, over and above all these, we might look for the blessing attached to every nation that humbly and faithfully obeys the behests [24] of God's Church. In this case, as in almost all other cases, there is no need for striking out a new path; the old one, that leads over the village green to the church door, is patent: our forefathers, that are at rest in the churchyard, used, in merrier or sterner days than ours, to frequent it – we have but to do the same. The wisest earthly policy that I know of is that which brings earth nearest to heaven, and *that* is to be found only in obeying the Church and observing her ordinances; and if, as in this matter of holy-days, the temporal and eternal welfare of the poor are equally promoted by her heavenly wisdom, what marvel? How great rather should be our sorrowful surprise, that, in spite of all our boasted enlightenment and liberality, we have despised the modest wisdom of old days, and are struggling in the helplessness of overgrown wealth and empty novelties; while all along the Church is witnessing to a purer and better age, and bringing us, if so be the whirl of money-making has not deadened our hearing, by many a rite and rubric, to listen to her gentle voice, and restore the poor and labouring population of England to her beneficent and venerable sway! She it is, and she only, that can knit together in the sanctifying bands of Christian joy and sorrow, of Christian fast and festival, the high and low, the rich and poor; – she it is, and she only, that can [25] bless the enduring toil of the husbandman or the craft of the mechanic, on earth, with glimpses of heaven. It was the Church that, in ruder but more humble times than these, arrested the sword of war by her blessed truce of God – it was the Church that then was the defence of the poor and the weak against the rich and the strong – it was the Church in later days that struggled for, and lost for the time in falling, the innocent mirth and recreations of the people – and it is the Church now that will restore to us, if we will accept the gift through 'her own appointed means and channels of grace,' the frankness and good humour, the strength and the glory of the old English character.

Shall we observe the holy-days of the Church?

(v)   The Revival of Urban Monasticism

Lord John Manners, *The Monastic and Manufacturing
Systems*[45]

> Sir Thomas More: 'And Which, Montesinos, Would, In Your Eyes,
> Be The More Melancholy Object Of Contemplation – The
> Manufactury Or Convent?'
>
> [Robert Southey, *Sir Thomas More*]

Chapter I

> Arise up, England, from the smoky cloud
> That covers thee; the din of whirling wheels:
> Not the pale spinner, prematurely bowed
> By his hot toil, alone the influence feels
> Of all this deep necessity for gain:
> Gain still; but deem not only by the strain
> Of engines on the sea and on the shore,
> Glory, that was thy birthright, to retain.
>
> Sir John Hanmer, MP[46]

Was the practical protest of Chartism, Infidelity, Dissent, and Socialism, which disturbed the kingdom last summer, to pass away, be a nine days' wonder, and then cease to be regarded and cared for?[47] Or is it to be remembered merely to justify the buildings of more gaols, the forging of more handcuffs, and increasing the police force, while the evils which produced that rough protest, and [3] against which it was entered, are to be overlooked and unreformed? We hope not; for that great and deeply-seated evils do exist throughout the whole of our manufacturing society we hold to be an incontrovertible fact; and men of all parties, from the Chartist to the agricultural Tory, admit the disease, though they quarrel about the remedy. For our own part, we have no hesitation in saying, that by and through the Church alone do we look for a permanent amelioration of those evils.

We believe that, as the misery and ignorance which caused these disorders sprung chiefly from the inefficiency of Church administrations and Church education, so do their remedies consist in what Mr. Gresley briefly and emphatically terms '*A Restoration of the National Church;*' but we also fear that the parochial system alone cannot, as at present constituted, fully provide for the spiritual wants of our manufacturing districts; and we hope to be able to show that it is not without reason we call for the foundation of religious houses.[48] In the first place, then, we would endeavour to lay bare the appalling spiritual as well as the temporal destitution of our large towns, in which we venture to say that Christianity is at a lower ebb than it ever has been in this kingdom since the invasion of the Danes. This is a melancholy subject, and we shall merely mention one or two [4] facts in corroboration of our statement: indeed, so much has been lately said and written on the subject, that we might think ourselves justified in assuming the premises, and only arguing to the conclusion, were it not that we wished to show the impossibility of Christianizing those huge hot-beds of Infidelity and Dissent by what is too generally understood to mean '*Church Extension,*' viz., the building of a certain number of churches, and appointing a curate to each, with the salary of an upper servant in a gentleman's family. Nothing is further from our thoughts than any attempt to depreciate that most beautiful feature in our Church – its parochial system. In the country, and in modest country towns, its excellence cannot be too highly praised or too vigilantly guarded. Nor would we dispense with it even in London and Manchester: but to it, in large overgrown towns, we would add a Monastic Institute . . . .

We shall dismiss, then, from our consideration, the deficiency which may exist in the country parochial system, as one that can be rectified without any great difficulty or important change [5] in itself, and proceed to show, chiefly from Messrs. Gresley's and Palmer's pamphlets, the impotence of that system, as it is now understood, to supply the religious wants of our large towns. Without entering into minute details and figures, we find, according to Mr. Palmer's calculation (which we have never heard disputed), that in 1841 seventy four parishes in London and its suburbs contained a population of 1,646,400, under the spiritual care of two hundred and twenty-one clergy; 'leaving (adds Mr. Palmer), in the metropolis alone, the enormous number of 1,425,000 people unprovided with spiritual aid, and requiring for their care upwards of one thousand four hundred clergy, in addition to the present ecclesiastical force of the metropolis.'[49]

'Take' (says Mr. Gresley)

> the example of Bethnal Green, which the excellent and indefatigable bishop
> of the diocese has made the scene of his special exertions. It is proposed to

build ten churches, in addition to the two now existing, for a population of seventy-four thousand souls, giving an average number of six thousand for each district. Suppose the ten churches built – what can one clergyman, even with an assistant, do in the pastoral care of six thousand souls? Each district of that magnitude ought to have an experienced pastor, of mature age, with five or six curates under him, if the ordinances of religion are to be rightly administered, and the people receive a proper pastoral superintendence.[50]

Let us take these two *minus* results of one thousand [6] four hundred clergy in the metropolis, according to Mr. Palmer, and of sixty in Bethnal Green, according to Mr. Gresley. Does not the very sound of these figures alone suggest the necessity of some sort of Monastic Institutions? Does any one in his senses really believe that Bethnal Green can support sixty clergy, living independently of one another; or that, if it could, such an arrangement would be desirable? In a district like that, now for long years the prey of Dissent and Infidelity, what is wanted and imperatively called for is the concentration, so to speak, of the Church's forces. No minute, no mite, ought to be allowed to pass away unemployed, or be expended uselessly; the strictest discipline and subordination should prevail among those who are to bring under the Church's rule a community so disorganized and undisciplined; each should co-operate with each other, and day by day strengthen each other with accounts of each day's diversified experience – the failures, the successes, the annoyances, the consolations of their Christian warfare. Every thought, every impulse of these Christian warriors should be weaned from the petty cares and pecuniary troubles of the world, and soul and body, the energies of the mind and strength of the limbs – all, all and like, should be devoted to their great work. But how can this self-devotion be [7] obtained or expected from men – from *gentlemen* – for be it remembered that now-a-days clergymen must be gentlemen, in the common modern conception of the word – weighed down with the difficulties of daily life, oppressed with the hundred petty cares and duties of work-day humanity, and perhaps doomed, after all their self-denial and painstaking to find, at the end of the year, their expenses exceeding their income, and themselves subjected to the scornful eye, the hasty word, the importunate demand of worldly trade?

Nor is it any answer to say that this state of trial and grief is favourable to the Christian growth of the individuals; undoubtedly it may be so, but how is it regards the district under his charge? For it is the spiritual destitution of the community, not the temporal destitution of the clergyman, that we are now considering. The fact may not be concealed, that the worldly isolation of a poor clergyman in a large urban district is most unfavourable to the success of his labours, not only from the causes we have already mentioned, but from others also; – for instance, in these days of curious research and prying knowledge, it becomes not only advantageous, but, in a manner, indispensable, for the minister of such a district to have ever at hand a storehouse of learning, whence, as occasions arise, he may draw forth the [8] weapon suited for the emergency – the dagger and pistol, bayonet, sword, or ancient battle-axe and heavy mangonel – else, how shall he successfully contend with the learned Romanist, the flippant Socialist, or the dogmatic Dissenter – all, it may be, in possession of their parts of the battle-field before his arrival? Would it be a slight assistance to such a man so situated to have ever access to a library in the very house he inhabits, consisting not of the few books which his own straightened means have allowed him to obtain, but of carefully-selected tomes, which public liberality or private munificence enable the society from time to time to purchase? But, perhaps, more important still would be the gain in alms-giving and charity – virtues, and privileged duties of the Church, which, we may be permitted to say, have become sadly secularized. Of old, we need hardly remind our readers, from the day whereupon the Church separated a new order of deacons for that very purpose, the duty of supporting the Christian poor was considered a Christian privilege; and it has been reserved for these our days to establish a system of national relief, which carefully excludes from its administration all that should bless alike him that gives and him that receives. But if we are anxious to wipe away this blot on our national escutcheon – if we are anxious to make our poor and needy brethren feel that they really [9] are our brethren in Christ – if, in short, we wish to unite all classes in love and mutual charity, we must do what in us lies to render the Church once more the great alms-giver in the nation; and how can this be effected, if not by the increased power and vigour of application arising from the concentration of funds in the hands of society? We believe that considerable sums are annually frittered away, from the want of some such organisation. Of course, this only applies to such districts as we have been contemplating; in rural parishes, on the contrary, the village priest should be the dispenser of charity; and we hope the day is not far distant when he will generally assume that character in a more marked manner than at present. We look to the revival of the Offertory for the best and safest remedy of the evils of modern Poor Law legislation; but in overgrown neglected town populations something more than the alms-dispensing of an unaided clergyman is required, and this is to be found in the co-operation of a *religious society*. This necessity is indeed so evident, that we need hardly point for proofs of it to the innumerable soup societies, cooking clubs, Dorcas societies,[51] &c., which every winter bear witness to the want of an efficient organisation, on the part of the Church, to meet the demands made on the charity of all her children. Great surely would be the gain to all classes were these [10] heterogeneous, and often competing societies, merged into one community, under the immediate and enfolding wing of the Church.

But in these latter remarks we have wandered into a consideration of the good that might be expected from the establishment of Monastic Institutions, whereas we intended in our opening to restrict ourselves to proving the want of them in large towns. This, we think, we have proved, in the case of Bethnal Green; and that which is true of Bethnal Green, is true also, in smaller or greater degrees, of Westminster, Manchester, Birmingham, Nottingham, and all towns wherein large masses of labouring and non-labouring poor have been collected together, nobody knows *how*, and been miserably neglected by Church and State, anybody may see *why*. If, then, in the preceding observations, and in what we shall say in the course of these chapters, we can show that some such institutions are now required by the Church's need, and are pre-eminently qualified to render her effectively the poor man's Church, in places heretofore almost entirely unblessed by her, we are justified, we trust, in urging this subject on the immediate and earnest attention of the Bishops of our Church, provided there be found no really weighty religious objection, which we truly think cannot be found.[52] [11]

Chapter II

Let us depart – these English souls are seared,
Who for one grasp of perishable gold
Would brave the curse by holy men of old
Laid on the robbers of the shrines they reared.

[John Henry Newman, *Lyra Apostolica*[53]]

Nothing is easier than to raise a cry of 'No Popery;' and we freely admit that any attempt to revive religious houses in England is peculiarly obnoxious thereto; but, entreating our zealous anti-popery friends to listen before they condemn, we proceed to examine into the justice or injustice, of such an accusation. And here, perhaps, we may remark, in passing, that this charge of 'Popery' has, since the Reformation, at various places and times, been brought against well nigh not every primitive, but also every

Christian doctrine and practice; and that, therefore, in itself, it is not worthy of any consideration; but the character of many who advocate it eminently deserves our respect and forbearance. In order, then, to remove any objections on the score of 'Popery', we proceed to quote expressions and opinions from various authorities – members, and [12] sound members too, of the English Church – favourable to a revival of religious houses, or strongly condemnatory of the wholesale destruction which overwhelmed them at the Reformation; and, therefore, if not exactly favourable by implication, at least not unfavourable to our views. To begin with the very Act that annihilated the lesser monasteries.[54] The preamble of that Act, after suggesting the propriety of suppressing all such houses as had been certified of less value than 200*l.* per annum, and giving them, with their lands and revenues to the king, proceeded 'to distribute their members amongst the great and honourable monasteries of the realm, where, thanks be to God, religion is well kept and preserved;' and granted to the king power to found anew such houses as he should think fit, by virtue of which, fifteen monasteries and sixteen nunneries were actually refounded, and remained until swept away again in the general destruction. Latimer, it is well known, never hesitated to express his sorrow at the wholesale ruin of those buildings, but with 'honest earnestness (says Southey . . .) entreated that two of three in every shire might be continued, not in monkery, he said, but as establishments for learned men, and such as would go about preaching and giving religious instruction to the people, and for [13] the sake of hospitality.'[55]

[. . .] After stating the various objections commonly urged against their boundless hospitality by the disciples of that just born science, now so potent in England – *Political Economy* – [Heylin] breaks out with: –

> All this is confessed; yet by their hospitality many an honest and hungry soul had his bowels refreshed, which otherwise would have been starved; and better it is two drones should be fed, than one be famished. We see the heavens themselves, in dispensing their rain, often water many stinking bogs and noisome lakes, which moisture is not needed by them (yea, they are the worst for it), only because much good ground lies inseparably intermingled with them; so that either the bad with the good must be watered, or the good with the bad must be parched away.[56]

Alas, alas! What is the state of education now among the teeming millions of our artisans? Grammar, and music, and Latin, what know the maidens of Dukinfield, or Staleybridge, of them?[57] What know they of that gentle instruction which woman, with sweetest, softest power, used to shed abroad among the hamlets of the rude north, not grudgingly, or of necessity, but freely, spontaneously, and without counting the cost? [20] . . . [I]s it too strong an expression of Mr. Paget, that our once happy country is turned into an aceldama of anarchy and irreligion?[58] . . .

The exceptions are so slight, that we shall not transcribe them. Comment on such a picture were superfluous! Turn our eyes which way we will, the same melancholy truth presents itself to our view; on all sides are huge masses of our fellow-countrymen – dare we say fellow-Christians? – growing up in worse than heathen ignorance, [21] and demanding from us, in language we may not understand – the language of Infidelity, Chartism, and Socialism – an immediate reception into Christian civilization.[59] . . .

. . . [T]he fearful nature of the evil being demonstrated and acknowledged, its fruits being tasted in the insurrection of last year, the inadequacy of our present parochial system to meet the evil being notorious, it becomes the duty not only of every Churchman, but also of every Englishman, to consider whether, in the event of a rational expectation being held out that by a revival in some sort of Monastic Institutions, that evil would be grappled with successfully, the religious objection to such a system is so strong as to forbid the trial being made. In the quotations we have so freely made from writers who have adorned the literature and practice of our [22] Church since the Reformation up to our own days (and we need not say with what ease these quotations might have been swelled into a volume), we have endeavoured to show that no such *a priori* objection can be maintained; but that, on the contrary, we are at liberty, with Archbishop Leighton, no Romaniser surely, to declare the destruction of the monasteries 'to be the great and fatal error of the Reformation,' and to say, with Mr. Paget: –

> If the monasteries, instead of being *swept away*, had been REFORMED – had been reserved for persons NOT TIED by MONASTIC VOWS, but who, satisfied to endure hardness, and content with poverty, were ready, from the pure love of God, to devote themselves to preaching, study, and prayer, our large towns would have been supplied, not as now, with some three or four overburdened clergymen, but with a numerous body of men ready, *under Episcopal guidance*, to do the work of Apostles and Evange-lists to multitudes (the expression is not too strong) now lying in darkness and in the shadow of death.[60] [23]

Chapter III

Whether our ladies might not as well endow Monasteries
as wear Flanders' lace?

[Bishop Berkeley, *The Querist*][61]

We shall endeavour, in the remaining part of these chapters, to show, what indeed may be fairly deduced from many of our proceeding observations, that there is fair ground for believing that the establishment of such institutions would meet the wants of the case; and shall conclude with pointing out a way for their speedy foundation and endowment.

Let us suppose, then, an 'ecclesiastical factory' (to use Mr. Frederick Faber's expressive term[62]) established in Ashton, or Staleybridge, with its, say ten, religious and ten lay brethren, animated by all the noblest and purest feelings that can act upon human nature, oppressed and drawn down to earth by no self-regards, having no opposition to encounter, save that (God knows, it is an opposition weighty enough) which past neglect throws in their way – let us fancy them baptizing the babes, instructing the young, frightening the [**24**] impenitent, consoling the afflicted, blessing the marriage-vow, superintending the distribution of alms and oblations among the needy, and carrying into every cabin and to the side of every loom the holy ministrations of the Church; going in and out among the people as the ambassadors of Christ, and the assertors of their inalienable rights as members of his Church; let us picture to ourselves the gate of their house, or abbey, or college (call it what name you will), thronged with the poor, the desolate, the oppressed (as the kingdom of heaven, which the Church here upon earth is dimly to foreshadow, will be thronged), while the brethren themselves, disciplined and strengthened by obedience, and schooled by each day's fresh experience, draw to themselves, and ultimately to that Church whose servants they are, and to the religion they profess, the love, and respect, and loyalty of the now degraded and seditious artizans. . . . [**25**]

But there is still another point to which we wish to direct our readers' attention. Great as would be the blessings which would arise to our benighted manufacturing population from the establishment of such religious houses as we have described, there is still another element in the charitable constitution of the Church which we much desire to see brought into play. After all that has been said and done on this subject – after Mrs. Fry's exertions, and Lady Isabella King's marrying nunnery at Bath[63] – it does indeed seem to us an extraordinary thing that the goodness and zeal, the charity and activity (not always, to be sure, very well applied), which animates so many visiting, clothing, and teaching ladies' societies, should never have bound themselves up for a trial, at least, in some methodical form. To take the lowest example of all – the class on whom Mrs. Fry proposes to work – the public nurses; what calling would be more illustrious, more full of peace here, more preparative for joy hereafter, were it but sanctified by religion, and entered into and persevered in for the unselfish and unpaid love of God and man? But now, when money is the reward, and charity is degraded into traffic, [27] how entirely has that calling lost, even in the eyes of the world, the beauty and fair name it once possessed? We are not much in the habit of holding up France, or modern French sayings and doings, to admiration, but in this matter we have a painful pleasure in awarding to that nation our just meed of praise; for that when the revolutionary madness of 1830 impelled them to banish all monastic institutions from their land, wisdom and humanity had still sufficient sway over the public mind to procure an exception in favour of the Sisters of Charity, who now discharge their functions in all the hospitals of that country with a self-denying, retiring, constant zeal, far above all human prose – far above all human reward. We defy anyone, though never so impressed with what is called the truly British conviction that everything in France must be wrong, to visit one of the large French hospitals, managed, as they are, in every minutest particular, by *les Soeurs de Charité*, and to leave it without confessing how infinitely preferable is the system which trusts the wounded and the ailing to the fostering care of religious charity, to that which, as in England, raises an altar to Mammon even in the very temple consecrated to Mercy. How many discontented, [28] avaricious, gambling old maids, faded beauties, speculating widows, have, during the last three centuries, in England, wasted their energies, and died miserably, because the 'great and fatal error' of the Reformation left them no scope for usefulness; while the world, seeing the Church set no store by their services, claimed them as its own, and bound its hardly-gilded chains round their souls and bodies! What an incredible sum of money, what industry, zeal, and talent, which might have been 'doing the State some service,' since the rise of our cotton manufactures, have been sunk, through no fault of theirs, by the ladies of England at the card-table, or the milliner's! Oh! shame to us, shame to our laws, shame to our Church, if we suffer this disgrace to our national religion to remain any longer – if we, by our senseless sneers and fatuous indifference, compel all the most exalted attributes of the female character to subserve any ends rather than those for which they were granted by a God of mercy, those of religion and piety. Away, then, with the coldhearted worldly objections which would grudge to spare a soul from the service of the God of this world. Let us have courage to say what many [29] think, and ask, in behalf of the desolate, demoralized, heathen population of manufacturing and toiling England – in behalf of her ten thousand daughters who are now dragging on their lives in a listless or fretful subjection to the world – in the name of a suffering humanity, and an enfeebled Church, that the Sisters of Charity may once again appear as angels of light and mercy in the streets of our dingy wealth-worshipping towns. . . .

But before we quit this interesting subject, which will, we are convinced, ere long force itself, by the course of events, on the attention of all Churchmen and Statesmen, all who care, though never so little, for their country, we must guard ourselves from the possible imputation that we wish to restore, in all its full-blown pride, the monastic system of the fifteenth century. The state of England at this time would alone afford a sufficient answer to the understandings of thinking [30] men; but, to prevent all possible misconception we emphatically declare that nothing would induce us for a moment to entertain the idea of the revival of monastic institutions, unless with the most unqualified assertion of Episcopal control, their entire subordination to the Church, and the absence of vows. As assistants to the parochial clergy, as servants and handmaids to the Church, we believe, and think we have proved, their existence would be most beneficial. Independent of the parochial clergy, and only perfunctorily supervised by the Bishops, it needs but small discernment to foresee that they would, even without vows, again split on the selfsame rock against which they were dashed in the sixteenth century. This, then, would be our pledge and their safeguard – subordination to the parochial clergyman, obedience to the Bishop, and the power of returning to the world, when the weakness of the flesh, or the hope of being more serviceable to mankind, inclines the individual to do so. If we do not enter into more minute details, it is because we hold them unimportant in themselves, and feel assured that, when once the Bishops have calmly considered and approved of such a step, they will most easily and inoffensively be supplied; while the three great checks we have mentioned will [31] prove an ample guarantee to the lover of pure and simple religion, that in advocating, as indispensably necessary to the present awful wants of our Church and nation, such a revival of the system, due care is taken to prevent a repetition of those disorders and excesses which were the accidents, and not the necessary results, of our former monastic institutes.

We now come, in the last place, to consider the most likely means to obtain the foundation and endowment of such charitable societies. It has been a growing fashion of late years to look, almost exclusively, to the

House of Commons for direct aid and interference in all matters relating to the Church; direct pecuniary grants have been demanded from that quarter for the purposes of Church building, education, and so forth; while, on its part, that Honourable House has not been slack to avail itself of the opportunities afforded by such requests – not indeed to grant them, but to alter this ecclesiastical institution, to abolish that bishopric, to pare down this deanery, and, in short, to exercise an unlimited sway over the temporal affairs of the Church.[64] Now, we have no wish whatever to put it still further in the power of the State (*i.e.*, in that of the House of Commons) to interfere with the [32] Church, and therefore it is that we at once put out of the question a vote of public money; although, of course, if a bright light were to break in upon Mr. Hume, Lord John Russell, or Sir Robert Peel, and show them that a monastery, with its religious guardians of public morality, or an hospital, with its religious superintendence, would be a cheaper as well as more efficacious medium of preserving peace and order than new model prisons, or a *gendármerie* constructed on the most approved continental plan, we should not offer any violent opposition to their acting thereupon; but still we ask not that from them.[65] Nor, again, would we have fancy fairs held, nor guinea soliciting cards sent out to rival the patriotic exertions of the Anti-Corn Law League, nor even sermons preached to raise a fund for this purpose. The course we would humbly but earnestly recommend is one which we are glad to hear some of the Bishops now advocating – a repeal or modification of the Mortmain-law of 1736: a law which, we confidently assert, never would have become the law of the land if an opportunity had been afforded of the Church's voice in convocation – a law which was protested against by both the Universities and by nearly every charity in the kingdom – a law based on views of policy the [33] most grovelling and unchristian, supported by arguments the most flimsy and ridiculous, and attended, in the whole course of its operation, with the worst and most disastrous effects.[66] . . . Let Sir Robert Peel . . . strike off the fetters wherewith a selfish generation has bound individual charity; let him bid fair scope be given to those who would fain leave their broad lands and fertile acres somewhat to the glory of God and the good of their fellow-men; let him take the initiative in leading the public mind of England back to a holier and more believing temper and course of action; let him call upon her Legislature to wipe away the mark of [34] Tyre, now so painfully stamped on her forehead, and replace it with the blessed sign of the Cross; let him do this, and, in addition to this, let him have the heart to suffer the Church of England to deliberate in convocation, and adopt such measures as shall seem to her meet and good for the present awful crisis of Christianity in this country; and we shall need no public grants for forming union district schools – no Queen's letters for alleviating gaunt distress – no rural police, nor fresh prisons. Private charity, which, in days gone by, built our glorious cathedrals, and founded our hospitals and monasteries, our schools and our churches, will again break forth for the salvation of the country. The first stroke of the trowel on the first religious house that is raised in Manchester will sound as the knell of anarchy; the first flutter of Mercy's white garment in the streets of Birmingham will scare away the spirit of revolution. . . . [35]

Political excitement has waned before the dreadful reality of a famished and heathen manufacturing population. Men of all parties acknowledge that neither the ballot nor an extended suffrage will feed or Christianise the hungry and the unbaptized; and the Government palliative of a comprehensive system of education will soon be found ineffectual for any but secondary purposes.[67] What is wanted is an energetic and powerful application of the Church system. This cannot come save through the establishment of a monastic system; and this, in its turn, can be obtained only through the repeal of the existing Mortmain-law. In Mr. Paget's words, 'Let the statute of Mortmain be repealed – were it but for ten years – and we should have churches and endowments once more, such as would be commensurate with the needs of our population.'[68]

To sum up as briefly as we can the thoughts that crowd upon us as we review the fearful dangers which beset our Church and nation, and the means that suggest themselves of escape. A huge mass of putrefying sores has been disclosed to the [36] eyes and hearts, not of our statesmen alone, but to those of all Europe – a mighty cancer, gnawing at the vitals of England, has been laid bare in all its hideous nakedness – the worship of Baal has produced its fruits; and the question, the only question to be considered, is, how are the people 'that sit in darkness and in the shadow of death' to be brought into the pale of Christian civilization? Away, then, with free trade theories, nicely balanced political systems, the cant about the rights of man, and the whole jargon of Liberal philosophy! Remains there on this earth a power to effect this great good other than the Church of Christ? No! Literature and science, wealth and commerce, liberty and license, have each and all put forth their strength, and reigned for their little hours.[69] How they have failed we now see and feel. To the Church, therefore, and to the Church alone, must the statesman, in this hour of danger and distress, look for consolation and safety. Wise in the experience of well nigh two thousand years, she still retains in her celestial armoury, if her wayward children will but let her use them, the weapons that can yet discomfit and destroy the hydra evil of our days. She still can wield, if so be the State is crafty enough to permit her, the sword that shall cut through the gordian knot of [37] our manufacturing misery and crime; for surely, if ever faith may believe that God suffered the monastic system to be founded for the benefit of mankind – if to any state of society that system be applicable, now is that time – ours is that state. We, at least, can see no other favourable solution of the appalling problem; and if we are driven to despair, and condemned to give up all hope for our country, it will be by hearing the views we have imperfectly, but honestly, put forth in these pages, derided as visionary, or denounced as Popish. But we would fain hope better things. Ever and anon, amid the howlings of the storm, is heard the low musical voice of the Church, speaking now from the episcopal palace in a tone of command – now issuing from the cloister in the accents of entreaty, and about, we trust, to sound trumpet-tongued even in the Senate: and so long as that voice, coming up from the tomb of the past, can yet stir men's minds, and encourage them to action – so long as God, in His wondrous mercy, still suspends the vengeance which we can almost see ready to fall on us, so long will we iterate our convictions on this subject, and pray to be permitted to see the charity that 'covereth a multitude of sins' dispensing freely, and without hindrance, her gifts and graces among a long-neglected and [38] toil-worn people; while the Church and the Hospital, the Monastery and the College, are sending out into every dark corner, into each concealed abode of sorrow and of sin, the messengers of salvation, the ambassadors of their Lord. Then, indeed, might we hope to see piety and peace once more flourish among us – fair freedom to be unpolluted by license – loyalty again to be an acting principle in the English mind, and England once again wear, and merit to wear, her fond cognomen of 'merrie;' for then would wealth have lost its arrogance, and poverty its disgrace, while the land of heroes and of saints would rejoice in a State which encouraged it to be Christian – in a Church which taught it to be happy. [39]

Lord John Manners, *The Laws of Mortmain*[70]

MR SPEAKER, . . .

It is impossible, Sir, I think, for any one seriously to consider the actual condition of this country and of Ireland – to see the millions of people who are suffering the extremes of want, and misery, and ignorance, and then to ask himself what has been done during the year 1843 by Parliament to ameliorate their condition, without sorrowfully and with shame confessing that, while no one has ventured to deny the awful existence of those most awful facts, nothing has been done to remove them. It is under these circumstances that I bring forward the motion; I bring it forward after – I say it more in sorrow than in anger – the sectarian bigotry of some, the blind selfishness of others, the want of moral firmness of a third party, have all conspired to defeat or render nugatory measures which might have been productive of good, and which would, at any rate, have been an earnest to the people that a practical good-will was borne to them in Parliament. It is only, then, after the House has declared that the ignorant shall not be taught, the starving fed, the unemployed set to work by public munificence, that I ask you to carry that principle to its full and legitimate extent, which alone can justify you in acting upon it; and while you refuse to be munificent as a State, to throw every facility in the way of individual zeal and charity, that they may effect what you will not do.[71] There is, Sir, one Gentleman in this House with whom I think these considerations will have weight – I mean the Right Hon. Gentleman, the First Lord of the Treasury [Sir Robert Peel]; from him I have more than once heard with the greatest pleasure expressions which encourage me to hope that the time is not far distant when restrictions on the exercise of charity and beneficence will cease to exist. ... [4]

... It is my earnest wish to afford practical encouragement to that individual exertion to which the Right Hon. Gentleman so truly said we must look; and it is for this purpose that I ask you to consent to my resolution, which declares the existing restrictions in Mortmain unnecessary.[72]

In order, Sir, to point out the restrictions which exist, and which I contend are useless and prejudicial, I shall be obliged to refer shortly to the origin and history of the Mortmain laws; and I trust I shall be able to show from that reference, that restrictions which might be beneficial in the fifteenth are altogether the reverse in the nineteenth century. In England, I maintain, restrictions in Mortmain originated in the natural dread which the great feudal barons, and each successive king, as the greatest landowner in the kingdom, entertained of the growing power and wealth of the monastic body: they were imposed, not from any political-economic notion that it was unwise to tie up land in perpetuity, but because, as is invariably alleged in the preamble of those Acts, such alienations to religious bodies deprived the lords of the advantages of tenure, and weakened the military defences of the country. ...
[5] ... But I contend that restrictions which were useful then, are useful no

longer. What reasonable ground of fear is there now of a fictitious title being set up by religious houses to lands which donors wish to grant to them? What reason is there now to apprehend detriment to the lords, or danger to the State, from tenants setting up crosses in their fields in order to avoid performing their proper military service? I think it, Sir, so obvious, that no argument in favour of Mortmain laws can be drawn, from enactments passed previous to the Reformation, from a state of society ecclesiastically and politically so different from our own, that I shall not weary the House by any further consideration of them. . . . [6]

But now, Sir, how different is the state of things! With six millions beyond the pale of the Church [7] – with at least a million of poor dependent for subsistence upon a form of charity which hardly deserves the name – when discontent and rebellion are rife in every quarter of the land, arising almost entirely from ignorance, misery, and destitution – . . . at a time and a crisis like this are we to be met with the cant and worn-out objection, that sound policy is averse to allowing lands to be held in perpetuity? – that it is unwise in any way to damp the ardour of commercial enterprize, and that therefore the Mortmain laws must be maintained? It will require, Sir, a considerable quantity of argument to convince me that the mere fact of a wealthy trader being allowed to leave his wealth, or the lands in which he may have invested it, to pious purposes, would necessarily indispose him or others to enterprize. But of this I am sure, that even granting such would be the case, we have little to fear on that score. The country is suffering far more from an undue desire of gain, and an excess of commercial competition, than it would suffer from any slight check which could be given them by the repeal or modification of the Mortmain laws.

Sir, I cannot believe that the arguments which were adduced in 1736 will be again pressed into the service. We surely shall not be told that it is impolitic to allow the Church to hold much land because her tenants must needs be effeminate and unwarlike, or because an ambitious Lord Primate might, through the power large Church property would give him, sway the destinies of the kingdom. I have heard, but I discredit the rumour, that I shall be met with the assertion, that [8] forty or fifty years hence the Church will be wealthy enough to Christianize the whole people of this country, and that therefore no change in the Mortmain laws is needed. Forty or fifty years hence, Sir, who will venture to say where we – where England herself may be before that? I entreat gentlemen who take so capacious a view of the subject to look a little nearer home – to think what the state of the people is *now*, what it is likely to be forty or fifty months, or even weeks hence, and to comfort themselves with the assurance, that if at that distant day every religious and charitable purpose be amply fulfilled, then they, or their successors, will be able without much difficulty to impose another statute of Mortmain. Sir, I dismiss all such considerations as utterly unworthy of serious discussion, and proceed to those which I apprehend will be the three chief objections urged against my resolution.

In the first place, no doubt, it will be said, that if restrictions are removed in favour of the Church of England, they must also be removed in favour of the Church of Rome and of Dissenters. Sir, I at once frankly avow that I am prepared to meet that objection, by denying it to be one. Roman Catholics and Dissenters are now on an equal political footing with ourselves; and by the 2nd and 3rd of William IV., on this very subject of Mortmain, we have acknowledged the right of the former, subject to our common restrictions, to build and endow churches, schools &c. I therefore at once say, that I seek for no special immunity for the Church. I am content that Roman Catholics should leave their wealth or their lands to build and endow schools and churches for the Roman Catholic population of the country; nay, I will go further, and say that high among the legislative boons which I think Parliament can grant to Ireland do I rank a revision of the Mortmain laws.[73] [9]

I hold this out to those who shrink back with anger and alarm from a proposal to pay the Roman Catholic clergy of that country. If you will not transfer the burden of supporting their priesthood from the shoulders of the miserable and ground-down peasantry of Ireland to the State, at least allow those of that persuasion, who are rich and willing, to bear the greatest portion of it; and permit Roman Catholic wealth to administer to the wants of Roman Catholic poverty.

I come now, Sir, to the second and most important objection, which urges that every possible precaution should be taken to secure the death-bed of a lingering person from the solicitations which may surround it. But a consideration of the state of landed property in this kingdom, a reference to the existing state of the law, and the slightest knowledge of the finer feelings of human nature, would, I trust, induce a conviction, that the fears which some entertain upon this head are, if not altogether unfounded, at least greatly exaggerated. . . . [10] Let any candid man strike a balance in his own mind between the possible evil of some one case of individual hardship, and the great probable – nay, certain – good which would result from a repeal of the Mortmain laws, and I would not hesitate to abide by the result. . . . [11]

I come now, Sir, to the last objection which I expect will be raised, an objection of a more positive nature than any of those I have yet noticed. I suppose it will be said, that since 1736 so many exemptions have been granted, so many charities have been allowed to receive lands, that every practical purpose is answered . . . . But, Sir, if this be so – if these exemptions are so numerous and so weighty, for what purpose, I ask, is the law maintained? . . . [12] If the law be so bad that you are continually exempting charity after charity from its operation, why retain it in the Statute-book? . . . Sir, of all mischievous legislation, the most mischievous is that which lays down a stringent rule, and then taxes ingenuity to break through and weaken it. What, Sir, is the obvious inference from these continual infringements on the inviolability of this law? The inference is plainly, that it is a bad law, which cannot be maintained; and I ask you, instead of frittering and juggling away piecemeal its restrictions, in a manner which increases beyond all belief the quantity of litigation, and gives security to no one, to remove it at once from the Statute-book. . . .

I have already pointed out the boon which such a step would confer upon Ireland, and from some observations which fell, on a former evening, from the Hon. Baronet, the member for Mallow, I conclude that his opinion coincides with mine on this matter.[74] But let us now for a moment look to England, and see if fresh inducements to charity, self-denial, and devotion, be not required among us. Sir, it is acknowledged that they are; schools, hospitals, churches, cathedrals are wanted; and in my opinion, beside and beyond all these, do we require the re-establishment of religious houses. I never can believe that the teeming millions [13] of our manufacturing districts are to be brought within the pale of Christian civilization without the establishment [14] of some sort of monastic institutions.[75] Call them by what name you please, but if the poor, the destitute, the ignorant, and the uncared-for are to be taught their privileges, no less than their duties, here – if they are to have bright hopes of an hereafter, as well as a sense of earthly happiness imparted to them, do not flatter yourselves that your Ecclesiastical Commissions, or your Endowment Bills, will alone effect that object.

I point out, then, a repeal of the Mortmain Act as the great means of endowing such institutions; but if the Church, by her authoritative voice in Convocation or Synod, were to decide that nothing should be done to educate and Christianize the untaught and miserable millions, save through the present parochial system, then I contend it becomes still more necessary to encourage and give facility to the foundation and endowment of churches, and colleges, and schools, by removing the present restrictions. . . . [15] I hope I have said enough to convince you that it is not without reason that I ask you to consent to my resolution. In an age confessedly devoted to money and money-getting –

when the wealthy are wealthier, and the poor – alas! that it should be so – are poorer in proportion than they ever were before – when hundreds of thousands are without food, employment, and religion – I ask you to have the courage to believe in the nobler impulses of our nature; to appeal to the glorious spirit which built our cathedrals, our colleges, our convents; to give scope to the exercise of those virtues, without which no country can become or remain great – faith and charity; and to brush away from the Statute-book the cobwebs which a faint-hearted and faithless age imposed for the purpose of entangling and fettering a munificence which they could not understand and did not love, and which we now mournfully desiderate.

Sir, I beg leave to move 'That it is inexpedient, in the present condition of the country, to continue the existing restrictions on the exercise of private charity and munificence.' [16]

Notes to Part II

1. The phrase was used as the title of the first chapter of Carlyle's *Chartism* (1839).
2. *House of Commons Debates*, 66 c306–6; moved in anticipation of the Hon. Charles Pelham Villiers' annual motion for the repeal of the Corn Laws.
3. A reference to the impact of Sir Robert Peel's 'free trade' budget of 1842 that abolished or greatly reduced a wide range of protective import duties.
4. A telling reference to the Prime Minister's father who had in 1819 introduced a bill to protect child workers in cotton mills.
5. See Francis and Morrow 1994, ch. 8.
6. Manners 1841.
7. Ibid.
8. Disraeli 1845, Bk I, ch. 3.
9. Young England (1845) 2 (11 January).
10. This speech is taken from the pamphlet publication (Ferrand 1841). Cochrane recalled that Ferrand's speeches on the Poor Law had a galvanizing effect on those who later formed the Young England party (Lamington 1906, pp. 151–2).
11. The parable is from Luke 16.19ff.
12. Perhaps a reference to a meeting held on 13 January 1840. An account by a participant mentions O'Connell's attendance but not the details recounted by Ferrand (Prentice 1853, I, pp. 142–7). Daniel O'Connell (1775–1847), the 'Great Agitator', MP for Kerry, was leader of the campaign to repeal the union between Great Britain and Ireland.
13. This phrase appears frequently in Young England statements; it seems to have been coined by Thomas Drummond (the Under-Secretary for Ireland in the Whig administration) in 1838 in response to a demand by Irish landlords for an increase in coercive measures by the government (Gray 1992, p. 32).
14. Richard Cobden (1804–65) was MP for Stockport. Having made a fortune in the cotton trade, Cobden was a leading figure in the Anti-Corn Law League; he was an obvious target for Ferrand.
15. Thomas Milner Gibson (1806–84) was active in the Anti-Corn Law League, following his conversion to free trade in 1839.
16. Richard Oastler (1789–1861), known as the 'Factory King' because of his role in campaigns to promote legislation limiting the hours of work in factories, particularly the 'Ten Hours' Bill'. A land steward in Flixton, Yorkshire, Oastler was dismissed from his position in 1838 because of his opposition to the introduction of

the 'new' poor law system in his neighbourhood. He was imprisoned for debt by his former employer; while in the Debtors' Ward at the Fleet Prison between 1840 and 1844 he published a periodical, *The Fleet Papers*.

17. This reference has not been identified, but Peel made a very similar point in a speech on working-class education (*House of Commons Debates*, 57 c215, 11.3.1841). The position expressed here reflects the stress upon personal responsibility that Peel derived from his theological views; see Hilton 1988.

18. *Kentish Observer*, 21 January 1841, reporting an election meeting held on 19 January during which Smythe had been criticized for not attacking the new Poor Law.

19. That is, Manners' father; see also Greville 1885, I, pp. 44–5.

20. *House of Commons Debates*, 70 c110–15.

21. Ibid., 68 c183–97.

22. Ibid., 71 c188.

23. Young England (1885).

24. *House of Commons Debates*, 73 c1396–1402. This speech, and the one that follows, were made in response to an attempt by the government to reverse a vote in favour of a Ten Hours' Bill.

25. Ibid., 73 c1416–21.

26. Ibid., 74 c1020–8.

27. Young England (1845) 12 (22 March).

28. Young England (1885).

29. Ibid.

30. Manners 1843b. Manners' pamphlet received favourable notice in the *Morning Post* of 10 January 1844 and the *Spectator* of 22 and 29 October and 10 December 1843. The motto is the Thirteenth Canon of the Church of England (1603).

31. Cf. Manners' speech at Manchester, below pp. 133–6.

32. The Opium War which began in 1839 was concluded by the Treaty of Nanking, signed on 29 August 1843; in September 1842 British forces reoccupied Kabul, having been forced to withdraw from the city in January of that year.

33. Manners refers to *The Book of Sports*, that is, *The King's Maiesties Declaration to His Subjects Concerning Lawfull Sports to bee used* (1618). Published originally by James I, this work was reissued by his son, Charles I, in 1633; the quotation in the text comes from p. 11 of this edition. Extracts from the work were reprinted in the appendix to the pamphlet.

34. This term is derived from Thomas Carlyle's *Past and Present*, Bk III, ch. 2, 'Gospel of Mammonism'.

35. Manners may have in mind the remark by Henry Phillpotts, Bishop of Exeter, who described 'pew rents' as a usurpation of 'the rights of the poor' (Soloway 1969, p. 274).

36. See Manners 1840, p. 579 and 1881, pp. 13–14 for observations of popular recreation and elite participation in Spain and Ireland.

37. That is, George III; for other examples of Manners' critical attitude towards Dutch influences in English life resulting from the Glorious Revolution of 1688–9 see 'William of Nassau', above, pp. 51–2, and Manners 1881, pp. 3, 9.

38. [Anon.] 1842, p. 251.

39. Manners and Smythe attended this church during their summer visits to the Lake District with their mentor, the Revd Frederick Faber; see Faber 1987, pp. 29–32, 38–40, 93–4.

40. Joseph Strutt, *Glig-Gamena Angel-Deod., or the Sports and Pastimes of the People of England* (1801). This illustrated work went through a number of editions in the

first half of the nineteenth century. Most of the illustrations depict medieval games; the text provides accounts of these as well as a history of the pastimes of both rich and poor in England. The newspaper titled *Young England* carried a regular column reporting on a wide range of sports and pastimes.

41. Cf. Manners, *The Monastic and Manufacturing Systems*; below, pp. 85–6.
42. Probably a reference to Faber's practice in his parish at Elton; see Faber 1987, pp. 95–7.
43. *The King's Maiesties Declaration*, pp. 7–8; Manners' emphasis.
44. See below, pp. 88–93.
45. Publication in pamphlet form under the pseudonym 'Anglo-Catholicus' of a series of articles that first appeared in the *Morning Post* on 23, 25, 29 March 1843. This newspaper gave strong backing to Young England. The motto, from Robert Southey's *Sir Thomas More: or, Colloquies on The Progress and Prospects of Society*, II, p. 242, is particularly appropriate. Southey (1774–1843), poet laureate and man of letters, was an early associate of Coleridge at a time when both men were hostile to the Church of England. After about 1812 Southey became a defender of the Church, stressing its role as an agent of social control and comfort for the lower classes. In the work cited he contrasts the social and spiritual achievements of the pre-Reformation Church in England with the neglect suffered by the poor under the 'manufacturing system'. He also stresses the benefits of patriarchal order (I, pp. 93–4, 105). Southey's work is the direct source of Manners' account of Protestant convents; see below, nn. 54, 66 and cf. Southey 1829, II, pp. 295ff. The juxtaposition of the image of the monastery with that of the 'manufactury' was central to A. W. Pugin's *Contrasts*; like Manners, he was inspired by Southey.
46. Sir John Hanmer, 'England' (Hanmer 1840). Hanmer (1809–81), a Whig MP, published a number of volumes of poetry. He and Manners were friends and shared an interest in promoting allotments for the working classes (Hughenden Mss, 106/1/fo. 10, Manners to Disraeli, 24.11.1843, and Whibley 1925, I, p. 160).
47. The summer of 1842 was marked by a meeting of the Second Chartist Convention in London; the rejection of its petition to Parliament was followed by a wave of strikes, most notably in the mill towns of Lancashire.
48. Gresley 1841. William Gresley (1801–76), a clergyman in the Church of England, was Prebendary of Lichfield. Gresley proposed a commission of inquiry into the condition of the Church and especially into the effect of a shortage of clergy on the fulfilment of its pastoral functions. Manners addresses this issue from a distinctive standpoint. Doubts about the efficacy of the parochial system were fuelled by a growing concern at working-class abstention from the Church's services. In response, efforts were made to increase the number of Churches, especially in rapidly expanding urban centres, and to increase the number of 'free seats' in them; see above, p. 70 and n. 35.
49. Palmer 1841. William Palmer, a clergyman, was a Fellow of Worcester College, Oxford.
50. Gresley 1841, p. 7.
51. Dorcas Societies were associations of church women making clothing for the poor.
52. Cf. 'The Young Generation', above p. 36.
53. Newman 1836.
54. That is, an Act of 1536; see Southey 1824, II, pp. 58–9.
55. Southey 1824, II, p. 71. Abridgments made at this point eliminate extensive quotations from Sir William Dugdale's *Monasticon Anglicanum* (1693); Thomas Tanner's *Nototia Monastica* (1695); William Camden's *Britannia* (1586); Thomas Fuller's *The Church History of Britain* (1655) and from Southey's *Book of the*

Church. These Protestant sources extol the educational, social and spiritual role of monastic institutions.

56. Manners refers to Peter Heylin's *Church History*, II, pp. 190, 191. Heylin, or Haylyn (1600–62) was an ecclesiastical writer with strongly royalist sympathies. The editor is unable to identify this work; the passage cited does not seem to come from Heylin's *Ecclesia Restaurata*, the most likely source of it.

57. Industrial towns in the Manchester area.

58. Francis Edward Paget (1806–82), a clergyman, wrote a series of tales presenting his views on Church and Social Reform. The phrase cited is from *The Warden of Berkinholt* (Paget 1843), p. xi. Paget's tale, addressed to the 'upper and middle ranks', dealt with : 'the responsibilities which rank, property, and education involve; the duties of the higher classes to the lower; the importance of other views and means of Christian Almsgiving, than those which satisfy the easy and selfish religion of the present day; the true principles of charity, and the difference between its judicious and injudicious exercise; the amount of luxury, folly, extravagance, covetousness, and selfishness existing . . . among all who adopt the received habits and modes of thought which prevail in modern Society; and lastly, the urgent need of great immediate and unshrinking sacrifice and self-denial on the part of us all, if we would provide . . . for the spiritual necessities of our teeming population; if we would stop the flood of iniquity which threatens to overwhelm us, and substitute Christianity, in our so-called Christian country, for the absolute heathenism into which great masses of the manufacturing districts are falling' (pp. ix–x). These aspirations were close to those of Manners, but he (and this might be taken as a hallmark of Young England) managed to address them with an earnest lightness of touch which is absent from Paget's jeremiad.

59. This argument echoes that developed by Carlyle in *Chartism*. Unlike Manners, however, Carlyle did not look to traditional ideas of political, social and ecclesiastical hierarchy to solve the problems blindly expressed by the working classes in their support for Chartism and socialism; see Francis and Morrow 1994, ch. 8.

60. Paget 1841, p. 59

61. [Berkeley] 1725, No. 453.

62. On Manners' relationship with Faber see above, pp. 3–4.

63. Best known as a prison reformer, Elizabeth Fry (1780–1845) also established an order of nursing sisters. Lady Isabella King's institution for women at Bath was discussed favourably by Southey 1829, II, pp. 305–9.

64. As, for example, in Anthony Trollope's *The Warden*, published in 1855, but set earlier in the century.

65. Joseph Hume (1792–1855), a radical MP who crusaded for reductions in public expenditure; 'retrenchment' was one of his watchwords. Lord John Russell (1792–1878) had introduced the Parliamentary Reform Act of 1832 to the House of Commons. He announced his conversion to free trade on 22 November 1845. Russell attempted to form an administration after Peel's resignation on 5 December 1845, but when he failed to do so Peel resumed office. In early July 1846 Russell succeeded Peel as Prime Minister.

66. See Manners' speech on Mortmain, below pp. 90–2. The inhibiting effect of the Mortmain Laws was noted by Southey 1829, II, p. 313.

67. This was originally a Whig objective promoted by Lord John Russell in the late 1830s; see Mandler 1990, pp. 183–92.

68. Paget 1843, p. 297.

69. Cf. *England's Trust*, below, p. 117.

70. Manners 1843c; the pamphlet publication of a speech made in the House of Commons on 1 August of that year (*House of Commons Debates*, 71 c99–109). Manners withdrew his motion (ibid., 71 c118). The term 'laws of Mortmain' refers to a series of Acts that inhibited bequests of landed property to religious foundations. Reference to the history of these measures, the most recent of 1736, is made in the full speech and in the abridgment of it printed here; see also Best 1964, pp. 28–31, 103, 107. The handling of legal material in this speech may reflect Manners' experience when he briefly read law before entering Parliament.
71. Manners refers to a range of frustrated initiatives made earlier in the year; he probably has in mind debates on Ireland; the condition of the poor; the Poor Law; the provision of allotments.
72. The 'Right Hon. Gentleman' is, of course, Sir Robert Peel, the Prime Minister; Peel's speech on education was made in the House of Commons on 28 March 1843 (*House of Commons Debates*, 67 c107–12, citing c108).
73. In a note inserted at this point Manners questioned the extension of the Mortmain Act to Ireland since that country had not been included within the scope of any of the relevant Acts. This issue was shortly to become a matter for controversy in Anglo-Irish relations; see Kerr 1982, pp. 131ff. The argument that a repeal of the Mortmain Acts would benefit Dissenters and Roman Catholics was made in a pamphlet by Christopher Wordsworth, Headmaster of Harrow School and a Canon of Westminster ([Wordsworth] 1845).
74. That is, Sir Denham Norreys, who spoke on medical charities on 15 March 1843 (*House of Commons Debates*, 67 c967–8, 970).
75. Manners inserted a long note at this point sketching the argument of *The Monastic and Manufacturing Systems* and referring readers to this pamphlet; see above, pp. 76–88.

Young England on Political and Social Culture

Underlying Young England's responses to specific parts of the 'condition of England question' was a demand for a fundamental transformation of modern social and political culture. Part III contains a range of material relating to this aspiration. Members of Young England called for the revival of a style of politics which took account of the promptings of the imagination. An independent and purified Church was a central feature of Young England's vision but its influence was to be felt within a political framework where aristocracy and monarchy would sustain the chivalrous ethos and the paternalistic values that were distinctive to them. But while Young England looked to the past for inspiration and for models of political culture, it did so in order to serve the needs of the present. It thus sought to integrate the commercial middle classes within a restored national community and attempted to apply its values to current political practice.

1 Feeling and Imagination in Politics

Young England maintained that a reliance upon narrow rationalism made it impossible to respond appropriately to the 'condition of England question'. It was argued that their contemporaries had undercut the basis for beneficial social order by discounting the political and social significance of feeling and imagination. In both their poetic writings and their contributions to contemporary political debate, Young England writers sought to convince their contemporaries of the importance of feeling and imagination and to restore these values to the centre of the political stage. The political application of this line of argument appeared most forcefully in Young England's contributions to debates on Anglo-Irish relations.

(i)   *Instincts of Loyalty and True Patriotism*

Alexander Baillie Cochrane, Speech on the Peculiar Burdens on Land, House of Commons, 14 March 1843[1]

[H]e was not one of those who considered that all expressions of popular feeling were to be despised, and that all combinations and associations for the promotion of political objects were to be [928] regarded in the same point of view; there had been conspiracies and insurrections against the established Government which must command respect from the deep conscious feeling which called them into existence, however much he might lament the instruments made use of, and the use to which they were applied . . . . We might lament the conduct of the Jacobites . . . but who could avoid sympathising with the devotion and the energy of those gallant spirits, who endured all, and sacrificed all, from a pure instinct of loyalty? . . . [**929**]

Alexander Baillie Cochrane, Speech on the State of Ireland, House of Commons, 7 July 1843[2]

. . . Government should in its measures take into consideration the feelings of the people of Ireland. Such feelings might be mistaken, but while they existed they should be attended to by Government. . . . The Irish character had not been sufficiently considered. It was noble, generous, and enthusiastic, easily excited to evil, but deeply sensible of kindness. On such minds one cold and unkind expression would inflict more pain than a long series of legislative favours would confer pleasure. Men of such character could not be harassed in vain; but he . . . did believe that if conciliation was properly tried, and not wrested by force . . . it would not be tried in vain. . . . [**749**] [E]ven the faults of the Irish arose from their excess of feeling, and even for their present errors he could find excuses. Patriotism is naturally an ardent feeling. What man can love his country with coldness? If we believe that moderation can combine with good faith, why may we not also believe that good faith can exist in men whose feelings lead them far beyond the grounds of due discretion? . . . [**750**] He would repeat, that nothing could save Ireland, but decision, energy, action, and affection. . . . If at the same time that we uphold the Union, and the principles upon which it was framed we cordially and frankly endeavour to win the sympathies and affections of the nation – if we [**751**] teach them that they have friends in this country who consider their interests – if while we are resolved to have the laws obeyed, we frame these laws as justly as possible – if we have real spirit of kindness and good will, which, even in a thousand unspeakable ways, and which, like the majesty of truth, carries conviction to all hearts – if landlords will discharge their duties to the land which Providence has bestowed upon them . . . then I do not despair of Ireland – I do not despair of one day seeing this nation, now so distracted and disaffected, a happy, united, and contented people. . . . [**752**]

Alexander Baillie Cochrane

(*From the Alexander Turnbull Library, National Library of New Zealand, Te Puna Mātauranga o Aotearoa*, ref no. S-L 195.)

(ii)   *Sympathy, Toleration and Justice*

George Smythe, Speech on the State of Ireland, House of Commons, 11 July 1843[3]

. . . [T]he difficulties by which the Government was at present beset, arose, not so much from Ireland as from England – from the Popery of Ireland, not so much as from the No-Popery of England. Some of our suburban pulpits were still disgraced by exhibitions which would be revolting if they were not ridiculous. . . . [919] But if this No-popery feeling had proved . . . an obstacle in the way of conciliation, he thought there was another no less formidable obstacle – he meant the perpetual Toryness of the policy of this country. It was much to be deplored that Mr. Pitt had been thwarted in his designs – it was untoward that he should have been driven to resign, as he did in 1802. It was untoward that the same attachment to the same question should have estranged Mr. Canning from his own political friends, and should have thrown a gloom over the last moments of his existence; . . . If that act had been passed by Mr. Canning, instead of the right hon. Baronet, he believed that the good that would have resulted from it would have been infinitely greater than had been felt. . . . [920] [H]e begged the House to recollect that the Government was not so much estimated by its intentions as by the feelings of sympathy which it manifested with the people, and it often happened that the slightest indication of good feeling was estimated in a high degree, and this was often observable from . . . almost the turn of a straw. . . . There were many means of comparatively small amount by which that House might show its sympathies with the people of Ireland. It was not generally known that the college of Maynooth was in debt.[4] . . . Now, he was sure that the Government would not think it a matter of reproach to take measures to do something more for that institution. . . . He knew that a feeling existed against that institution, and more particularly on his side of the House. He had heard with regret, hon. Members say, that the Maynooth priests were of the lowest possible popular extraction . . . . For one, he should not have the slightest hesitation to join issue as to the charges which had been brought against that institution. He thought that it was a fortunate circumstance that the priests were of this popular character, for he believed that priests for [922] the people should be of the people. This was his deliberate feeling and opinion. They were like the priests of La Vendée, where their parishioners might almost be regarded as the sons of the priests. If at the commencement of this century the Government had pursued the wise system of fostering the priesthood, and not adopted the beggarly system of doling out a paltry allowance to this institution – if they had carried out the wise designs of Mr. Pitt, by attending to this matter, in which the people were so deeply interested – if they had followed the example that had been set them elsewhere, the priests would have been found, as in the west of France, the advocates of order and peace, and the preventers of agitation and excitement. . . . [923]

Richard Monckton Milnes, Speech on the State of Ireland, House of Commons, 19 February 1844[5]

. . . [R]eligious ascendancy was the great root of all the evils which they had to deplore in the state of Ireland. It had been well said . . . that the Irish people were by far the most religious people in the world – that, even in the present incredulous age, they remained firmly and sincerely attached to the faith of their forefathers, and that they continue to be, as it were, a great remnant of the Middle Ages which time had left behind in its course. It was not then to be wondered at, if such a people should have a strong feeling against the religious ascendancy that was exercised over them. He would ask whether every young Member of the House who had spoken on the present debate, had not expressed somewhat of the same opinion as that which he then announced? and that might perhaps be accounted for by the supposition, that both in the House and out of it, young persons were enabled from particular circumstances, to see more distinctly than their seniors the causes of existing evil in Ireland. . . . It was utterly impossible, that they could expect to tranquillise that country while the present religious differences were kept up. . . . [**1162**]

2 Church and State

Young England's views on the political significance of feeling and imagination were related closely to their attempt to promote the complementary roles that they ascribed to the traditional church and state. In this, as in other cases, Young England writers took their models from the past. In the medieval period, and more fleetingly in the seventeenth century, church and state formed the core of a system of beneficial authority. Young England writers argued that it was to these models, and not to the Erastianism of recent practice, or the modern panacea of extensive popular representation in the House of Commons, that one should look for a solution to contemporary problems. It was assumed, however, that if traditional authority was to be made appealing and effective, the Church must join with the state in assuming responsibility for the social condition of the population.

(i) Church and State in History

Lord John Manners, 'England's Trust'[6]

I

'In returning and rest shall ye be saved; in quietness and in confidence shall be your strength.'

Isa. xxx. 15

The sun is slowly sinking, and the day
In changeful tints fades opal-like away;
The Earth melts into Heaven, and the breeze
Scarce hymns the vespers 'mid the rustling trees,
While all illuminated by the flood of light,
Wood, hill, and valley burst upon the sight;
And many an inland cove and sheltered nook,
Sequestered dingle, and meandering brook,
That 'scaped perchance the eye in mid-day's glare,
Now lie revealed in fairy colours there;
And stern and black before my raptured eyes,
St. Alban's hallowed walls in light arise. [1]
Ye holy towers! that, bathed in glory, stand
Like Guardian Angels of this Christian land;
From your old cloisters went in triumph forth
The voice that preached salvation to the North.
A thousand years since then, in strife and storm,
Have swept unheeded o'er your sacred form,
And now in varied tints the sunbeams fall,
On mouldering arch and desecrated wall;
Till Faith restores the glories of your prime,
And hails ye victors of decay and time!
Oh! who in such an hour but loves to soar
On Memory's wing to thoughts and dreams of yore,
To hold sweet converse with the well-loved dead,
And on the lands in youth he trod, to tread;
To feel old times return, and once again
Gay health and hope invigorate each vein?
Sweet dreams, sweet thoughts! and such are mine the while
I gaze upon yon old consecrated pile.
Ye holy towers! the angels guard your walls
With blessed ward – those deathless seneschals; [2]
Beneath your shade, in days of haste and toil,
'Mid struggling factions, and through parties' broil,
When thoughtful men half-sacred begin to view
In the fierce throes of changings ever-new,
Signs of the coming evening of the world; –
I love to snatch a contemplative hour
From vain pursuit of pleasure, fame, or power,

And from the ever-changing clouds of life,
Now bright in sunshine, and now dark in strife;
Lured by the solemn quiet of this shrine,
Its sacred spells, and influence divine;
Turn my tied gaze to some time-hallowed page
That sadly tells us of a nobler age,
When men of stalwart hearts and steadfast faith,
Shrank from dishonour rather than from death;
When to great minds obedience did not seem
A slave's condition, or a bigot's dream;
When Mother-Church her richest stores displayed,
And Sister-State on her behalf arrayed
The tempered majesty of sacred law,
And loved to reason, but at times could awe; [3]
When kings were taught to feel the dreadful weight
Of power derived from One than kings more great,
And learned with reverence to wield the rod
They deemed entrusted to their hand by God.

   Blest times! thrice blest, tho' treason's rebel-horde
Brought to the block a Strafford and a Laud,
Whom pitying Time had spared, tho' long his own,
And stained with gore the violated throne.
Still are those times to me most justly dear,
Tho' gentle Pity drops th' admiring tear;
Still do I love to learn from those who died
Rebellion's victims and their country's pride,
How to despise bold Reason's ceaseless din,
And reign omnipotent myself within.
Fast on the rock that has for ages stood
The tempest's howling, and the ocean's flood,
My faith in my dear Mother-Church I fix,
And scorn Religion's modern politics.
What, tho' no more her awful lightning's shine
To guide the wanderer to her sacred shrine;
Tho' statesmen deem they may with safety spoil
Those courts that prove their fathers' holier toil; [4]
While, sacrilege their path to future fame,
They glory in the deeds that stamp their shame,
Deep in that Church what treasures buried lie

Unseen, unlooked for, by the careless eye!
How gleam in each old half-forgotten rite
The magic rays of Apostolic light!
Oh! would her priests but dare to raise on high
Her glorious banner to the storm-rent sky,
Be bold to plead their Mother's holy cause,
Nor shrink from one least tittle of her laws,
Then might our England justly hope to be
What she was once – the faithful and the free:
Then might she, her meteor-flag unfurled,
Despite the threatenings of a banded world!
. . . [5]

(ii) The Restoration of Church and State

Lord John Manners, Speech on Parliamentary Reform, House of Commons, 18 May 1843[7]

He opposed the motion . . . differing . . . on the abstract principles on which he conceived the motion to be founded, – denying altogether the position [525] that the people were the source of all legitimate power, – believing, as he most conscientiously did, that all political power derived its only sanction and incurred its chief responsibilities from a source far higher than that abstract something or nothing – the people . . . . Furthermore, he conceived that as the principles he advocated were departed from, so the comforts of the people had diminished. For the last 150 years the principles contended for by the hon. Member for Rochdale had been more or less put into practice, and as power was taken away from the mitre and crown, and transferred either to the people in that House or out of it, their physical and moral happiness had been lessened. . . . He would extend the feeling of responsibility between the rich and the poor, and shorten the interval which in his opinion was growing too wide between those for whom wealth was made and those who made it for them. Thus they would most materially promote the welfare of all classes. It was because he was convinced that the happiness and prosperity of the people were intimately connected with the triumph of those principles –

principles which, as they demanded ready obedience on the one hand, involved the most serious and awful responsibilities on the other – principles which, while they would render the church triumphant, and the monarchy powerful, would also restore contentment to a struggling, overworked, and deluded people – that he opposed the motion of the hon. Member. [**526**]

(iii)   *The Social Role of the Church*

[Anon.], 'The Church and State, in Relation to the Poor'[8]

Questions relative to the doctrine or discipline of the Church are not proper subjects to be discussed in a public newspaper. YOUNG ENGLAND will leave such questions to be settled within the bosom of the Church herself. The Church, however, has other duties besides initiating to the faith, and expounding the doctrines of Christianity. Her temporal office is to carry into practice the principles of Christ's teaching in good works; by insisting upon the brotherhood of mankind as a reality; and acting as the universal pacificator and mediator between man and man. By taking upon herself these collateral duties, the Church justifies the maintenance of temporal power. The way in which she is enabled to discharge such duties, and the adequacy of the means placed at her disposal for that purpose, are matters of deep interest to society. There is no subject of equal importance so little understood in the present day as this; it will, therefore, be our duty to press it frequently and earnestly upon the attention of the country.

This is the more necessary at this time, when the puritan spirit of the middle class in our commercial town has, in a greater or lesser degree, influenced the catholic spirit of the Church Universal. When some of her members follow rather than lead the spirit of the age; and regard the Church too much as the propagandist of a particular creed, rather than as the instrument for developing the whole purpose of the Christian dispensation – a most important part of which is the duty of the rich in relation to the poor. . . . The Church, in its inception catholic and universal, is the siphon through which the superfluities of the rich should flow to relieve the necessities of the poor. Any law which obstructs the free flow of Christian munificence, limits the power of the Church to perform an important duty, and deprives the poor of a most valuable right. It is for this reason YOUNG

ENGLAND advocates the abolition of the LAWS OF MORTMAIN; and the removal of every other barrier which either law or convention have set up, between the poor man's wants, and the excess of the rich man's possessions.[9]

At the time when the property was taken away from the eleemosynary corporations attached to the Church, the struggle between wealth and poverty commenced, and it has gone on ever since; – its virulence increasing at a multiplying ratio. Every year has added more to the stock of the wealthy, and placed comfort at a great, and greater distance beyond the reach of the poor. Protected and fenced in by the laws which guard private property, the rich have had full command over the productive power of the poor. The right of the poor, to live in comfort by a fair quantity of labour, cannot be brought within written rules. It cannot be the subject of a *nis prius* verdict, or be realised by a writ of execution; – but must come from the *conscience* of the rich in the discharge of their social duties. Property, which has the security of the law and the executive, has been bargaining, for a long course of years, with labour; the boundary value of which, it is confessed on all hands, cannot be secured by a like protection; whilst the mediating and protecting influence of the State Church has been taken away. The consequence is, as might be expected, that a time has come when the two extremes of wealth and poverty stand face to face.

We know not whether it is the ambition of wealth, or the desperation of poverty, which seems most to menace a trespass upon our social organisation. The immense increase of wealth has induced class rivalry, at the one end; whilst the horrors of poverty have begotten class hatred at the other. The aristocracy of the money-bag is contending for position with the aristocracy of birth; whilst the peasant and artisan, who owe no allegiance to capital, feel in their degradation and their poverty, that the power which property holds for their protection is used as the instrument of their oppression. If the system goes on unchecked, there must soon be either too many palaces at one end, or too many workhouses at the other; in either of which cases the arch of society will 'cave-in' and social confusion will be its inevitable consequence.

We do not attribute this state of things solely and only to the Law of Mortmain, and to the Church being deprived of her temporal possessions, but we contend that by that policy the strength of the Church to curb the growing power of the rich has been weakened and her means of relieving the necessities of the poor have been taken away. As the law now stands, the Church cannot give to all classes, in the most efficient manner, the practical benefit of her influence.

[. . .] Superficial observers may think it matters little whether the poor are relieved in their necessities by the Church or by the State. Cold utilitarians may say that the workhouse soup satisfies the appetite as well as a meal eaten at the table which an ecclesiastical corporation may spread. They both may have the same effect upon the body; but upon the mind – the conscience – the soul of the man, their influence is totally different. The State professes no sympathy for the individual; but treating the class as a social incumbrance, it provides enough relief to avoid the commission of actual crime. . . . The Church in her benefactions feels for the sufferings of the man and acknowledges the claim of the brother. She supplies her aid in consideration of the intrinsic right of the individual, and not from any necessity which she feels to protect the rights of property by keeping a certain class above the desperation point.

The relief which the law provides is accompanied by every variety of circumstance which ingenuity can suggest to make it repulsive to the recipient. It is associated with an idea of class degeneracy, and surrounded by forms of individual degradation; and has a permanent influence in depressing the spirit of the receiver by ranking him as a pauper. The thought that he has joined a prescribed class sinks deep into his soul, and destroys that self-respect which is so necessary for the maintenance of manly feeling.

The recipient of alms from the Church, on the contrary, is taught to believe that he is assisted to find his place at nature's common table, which he seemed for a time to have lost. The only ceremony is, that he should join in the general thankfulness. His equality in the eye of God over all is recognised, and his individual self-esteem is preserved. The necessity of the poor calls forth but an acknowledgement of a right . . . .

Let it not be said that the statute-book of this Christian country contained an act which limited the power of the rich to be bountiful to the poor through the glorious channel of a common faith, and that the young and generous spirits of the age pleaded its abolition, and pleaded in vain. Above all, let it not be said that this boon to the poor was refused because sectarian prejudice had greater weight with a British legislature than Christian charity. [**106**]

(iv) *The Dangers of Erastianism*

George Smythe, Speech to the Conservative Electors of Canterbury, 1847[10]

. . . The next subject to which I should wish to advert, is the question of Education. I am bound to say I looked with little satisfaction on the scheme proposed the other day by Lord John Russell.[11] It think it was meagre as a [13] measure of State, and offensive as a matter of religion. I think that it conceded what, to all intents and purposes, amounted to a monopoly to that established Church which has, by the confession of the best and wisest of her ministers, been guilty of neglecting, for certainly more than a century, her most sacred duty, that of teaching her own children. And why has she been guilty of this? Because she is lying bound down and fettered in the lowest dungeons of Erastian imprisonment – because she has been compelled to accept the alms of the State without its confidence; moneys upon moneys, but at the same time disfavour upon disfavour.[12] The Church of England since the year 1800, has received 5,000,000*l*., but concurrently with those 5,000,000*l*. every token of aversion and discountenance – check upon check, discouragement upon discouragement, disfavour upon disfavour – the annihilation of all the old bulwarks of uniformity – the repeal of the Test Act, of Roman Catholic disabilities, the endowment of religious creeds alien from her own. I am sorry then that before she has had the time, and before she has done very much to gain public confidence, another of these fatal gifts should have been forced upon her, which only gain her abuse, hostility, and reactionary hate. I agree so far with the assertion of Mr. Roebuck, that sufficient cause has not, as yet, been shown against a large and comprehensive measure of secular education.[13] For I hold that all schemes with an admixture of religion must necessarily, I fear, more or less injure the rights of conscience, and wound the feelings of Dissenters. I know that in an archiepiscopal city, like Canterbury, this cannot be a popular sentiment. I know that there are many to whom the very word Dissenter is a stumbling-block and scandal. I can only say I have no such feeling. Why I know enough of history to tell me that Christianity itself was at one time dissent; when Pagan Rome was an established religion! I admire, as no unmeet sequel to the long-continued and serial magnanimity of their nonconformist forefathers, under all the vexatious oppressions of [14] Uniformity and occasional Conformity Bills,[14] the spirited resistance of the Dissenters to this unjust, partial, and sectarian measure of Lord John Russell.

But some may ask why, with these opinions, did you not vote against the measure? I tell you frankly, because I believe the want of education is so crying in this country, that any scheme of education, even this scheme, with all its vices, was better than none at all.

There is another subject which has been frequently and much canvassed of late – the endowment of the Roman Catholic priesthood in Ireland. I am in principle opposed in this our time to the general endowment of religions. I will not say to the partial payment of all religionaries, for there may arise particular, or provincial, or colonial cases of necessity; but in principle I am an opponent to general endowments. In the old days, the priest was thought by the public to be the representative of truth, and the State, its vicar, consequently and logically enough, punished Dissenters as it would have punished criminals. In these days, the priest is thought to be the representative of heaven, and the less he has to say to the earth, or its minerals, the better. The Irish priesthood, for example, are especially and eminently what Napoleon called them – the moral captains of the people. But why? Only because they are independent and unpaid. Endow them, and they will lose their influence; that is my deliberate opinion. . . . [15]

3   Aristocracy and Paternal Government

A responsible aristocracy and a paternal system of government were central components of a revived social and political culture. In their historical writings Manners and Smythe used recent French and English experience to provide exemplars of an appropriate aristocratic ethos. The histories of these countries also furnished salutary examples of aristocratic corruption, of the dangers of divisions between the aristocracy and the monarchy, and the dire consequences of challenges to royal authority.

(i)   *The Lessons of the English Past*

Lord John Manners, 'England's Trust'[15]

III

As some Spring-flower, that long beneath the earth
In patience bides the fated hour of birth,
Then, gently budding, lifts its tender head,
While, slowly opening, all its beauties spread;
Called by the balmy breath of Spring, it owns
The call, and opens at its dulcet tones; –
So now the purer faith of purer days
Peeps through the mould that hides the good old ways,
And struggling through this chilling age's gloom,

Gives fairest presage of a glorious bloom.[14]

. . .

Then did each high hereditary lord
Sit at the head of his own princely board,
Where sate the stranger, and the menial crew,
Who owed him fealty and affection too;
But if his wayward temper ill could brook
Or hasty answer, or irreverent look, –
If lust, or pride, or hatred moved his breast,
God's priest was there to do his lord's behest,
And haughtiest kings have stooped to kiss the rod
Wielded by some poor minister of God.
Each knew his place – king, peasant, peer, or priest –
The greatest owned connexion with the least;
From rank to rank the generous feeling ran,
And linked society as man to man.
  Gone are those days, and gone the ties that then
Bound peers and gentry to their fellow men.
Now, in their place, behold the modern slave,
Doomed, from the very cradle to the grave,
To tread his lonely path of care and toil;
Bound, in sad truth, and bowed down to the soil,
He dies, and leaves his sons their heritage –
Work for their prime, the workhouse for their age. [16]
Such is the boon that Independence brings,
That most deceitful of all tempting things.
Hail, Independence! who can number all
The blessings rare that answer to thy call,
And by a stroke of thy enchanter's wand,
Enrich each peasant's hut throughout the land?
Lured by thy light, the working classes own
No sickly love for Church, or State, or Throne:
Th' enlightened booby feels the generous heat;
Disdains to own dependence on the great,
And learns to murmur at his low estate.
But justice bids the lash of blame to fall
On rich and poor, on great as well as small.
Oh! would some noble dare again to raise
The feudal banner of forgotten days,

And live despising slander's harmless hate,
The potent ruler of his petty state!
Then would the different classes once again
Feel the kind pressure of the social chain,
And in their mutual wants and hopes confess
How close allied the little to the less. [17]
Oh! that the Church would bid the helpless know
In Her the sure reliever of their woe,
And vindicate the claim She erst possessed,
The care of all the lowly and oppressed! . . . [18]

  Must we then hearken to the furious cry
Of those who clamour for 'equality?' [23]
Have not the people learnt how vain the trust
On props like that which crumble into dust?
Are the gradations that have marked our race,
Since God first stamped His likeness on its face,
Gradations hallowed by a thousand ties,
Of faith and love, and holiest sympathies,
Seen in the Patriarch's rule, the Judge's sway,
When God himself was Israel's present stay,
Now in the old world's dotage to be cast
As weak pretences to the howling blast?
No! by the names inscribed in History's page,
Names that are England's noblest heritage,
Names that shall live for yet unnumbered years,
Shrined in our hearts with Crecy and Poitiers,
Let wealth and commerce, laws and learning die,
But leave us still our old Nobility! [24]

(ii)   *Aristocratic Grandeur and Hubris in French History*

George Smythe, 'The Aristocracy of France'[16]

The aristocracy of France is the most illustrious that the world ever saw. There
may be more ancient titles in Scotland or in Germany; more arrogance of

George Smythe

(From the Alexander Turnbull Library, National Library of New Zealand,
Te Puna Mātauranga o Aotearoa, ref no. S-L 193-A.)

descent in Italy or Spain, more gentle blood in our own old manor houses of
Northumberland or Lancashire; but no aristocracy can compete with hers in
sustained and European illustration. The very vice of the system was the cause
and continuation of its brilliancy. The nobleman of the ancient regime was
born to the high places of the army and the state, as with us he is born to his
hereditary possessions. The baton of a Marshal, the seals of a Minister, the
government of a Province, devolved almost as surely as the heraldic quarter-

ings upon a shield, or the seigneurial rights of an estate. The doctrine of 'the aristocratic succession' was upheld with a religious pomp, and a more than religious intolerance. It was not so much an order as a hierarchy. It [7] was a hierarchy based upon exclusion, and rule, and form, and caste. It had its army, its navy, its law, its church, and its finance, – all patrimonies rather than professions. [8] . . .

. . . Idleness was not the condition of a title, a luxurious ease not the privilege of rank. The nobleman who claimed the immunities, claimed also the labours of the state. Its great offices were not for the few, but they were never performed with more of personal activity than by grandees like the Le Telliers, and the Choiseuls.[17] The young patrician who was so insolent to the pekins of the bourgeoisie, would allow no one else to fight for them but himself. It would be unfair to try him by our stricter standards of obligation and morality. There was a wild patriotism at the bottom of all his recklessness and bravado. He did his duty to his country, but he would do it in his own way. He did not conquer the less because he hummed the gayest air of the last opera, or smoothed a perfumed ruffle, amidst the roar and danger of the battle.

It must also in fairness be acknowledged in favour of the French aristocracy, that it would have been impossible in any other country to have ensured, out of so small a field, so limited a choice, such great and dazzling services. The old idea of honour supplied the want of a larger and public competition. But it would be wrong not to point out the natural [11] consequences of this exclusive and formulary narrowness of system; the inveterate ingratitude, the consummate perfidy, 'the vicious perfection' of sectarian selfishness, which were its results. It was a sense of this truth, which accounts for Louis XVIII's almost invincible reluctance to consent to an hereditary chamber.[18] A slight glance at history will confirm the wisdom of his opinion. . . .

When Richelieu ordered the Constable de Montmorenci, notwithstanding his name and achievements, to be beheaded, – when de Bassonpierre, the companion-in-arms of Henry IV., was dragged by his commands to the Bastille, he was influenced by no capricious, or unneccessary cruelty. He was carrying out, by [12] determined means, a determined end. Upon his attaining the ministry, he found the king only the first of his nobles. He resolved to make him something more. He undertook to concentrate all the power, which he saw dissipated among many great Feudatories and Lords. His first care was destruction, his second centralization. His first object was to break the cisterns into which the waters had been gathered; his second to direct and receive them in one fountain head. His design was eminently successful . . . .

But not satisfied to dedicate his own life to this object, he devolved his power upon a successor, whom he himself had formed, who was instigated by the same motives, and who, sprung like himself from democracy, inherited, with instinctive zeal, his hatred, and his views [13] of Aristocracy. But the character of Mazarin was less firm than that of Richelieu; it inspired the great lords with hope, – he sought to govern by dividing, rather than by crushing them. The Rebellion of the Fronde broke out.[19] It was the last effort of Feudalism to rise against the far-sighted Oppression, which was destroying it. And, at its close amidst the ruin and exhaustion of so many princely fortunes, the decay and wreck of so many ancient houses, there arose the strongest executive that the world ever knew, the monarchy of Louis XIV. Thus it was in the demolition of an Aristocracy that the foundation of the Monarchy was laid.

But the sagacious policy of the two Cardinals, was not destined to be continued by the great King who they had made. He took pains in nothing so much as in rebuilding what they had pulled down, in raising up what they had so skilfully destroyed. The ancient races of France had disappeared. But all that splendour and magnificence which had belonged to the Dukes of Burgungy and Guienne, the Counts of Flanders and Thoulouse, he delighted to revive for flatterers and mistresses, and valets. . . . [14]

The fatal system thus blindly founded by Louis XIV. was recklessly adopted by his successors. The Regent – of the House of Orleans between which and the Middle Class there seems some mysterious tie – carried honours and dignities into the very heart of the *bourgeoisie*. Less generous than his predecessor, he sought not so much to enrich as to ennoble. The Bourse and the Rue Quincampoix were deemed worthy to give their illustration to the Aristocracy.[20] The Parliamentary families were summoned to participate in his lavish degradation and profuse abasement of rewards. But the reign of Louis XV. was to bear the palm from both these different excesses of abuse. He gave orders upon the Treasury to as many courtezans as Louis XIV. He gave patents of nobility to as many *roturiers* as the Regent. [15] . . .

It is clear to the most superficial observer, who looks back . . . upon scenes of such extravagance, that no country could long support two such burdens as an absolute and profligate king, and an insolent and tyrannical aristocracy. But it is not so clear to simple and upright minds, that the first ought to fall by means of the last, – the benefactor through the intervention of the benefited. It is difficult for them to believe that a king can oppress his people, but not caress his nobles, with impunity. Yet such was the melancholy truth. It was not the poor and persecuted who were the instigators and leaders of the Great Revolution. That Clermont-Tonnerre who is inveighing with such eloquent indignation against class legislation, and the separation of the three orders . . . who is among the most successful antagonists of the Court, was descended from a country lawyer, whom the beneficence of the monarchs had raised to that influence, which he thus perverts to their ruin and destruction. That de Liancourt, whose house had received so [16] many and such signal tokens of the royal bounty . . ., who owed all his wealth and position, all his rank and possessions to the crown, was not ashamed, after the taking of the Bastille, to become the second President of the Constituent Assembly. That de Noailles, – whose name derives all its renown from royal favour and condescension . . . by the Bourbons, insulted their descendent by receiving him, on his forced return from Varennes, at the Tuileries.[21]

But why eliminate names from the list, when the whole catalogue is so black with treachery? Why dwell upon a stray passage, when the whole story of aristocratic ingratitude is so notorious. . . . Who has forgotten that the first to desert their king, to emigrate, were the nobility? . . . [17] But the more detestable policy has never been sufficiently branded, which, in its refinement of selfishness, animated the aristocracy to second the worst efforts of the populace, to push them to extremes, to goad them to excess, careless of any outrage to their king, reckless of any danger to his person, in the hope that, out of an exaggerated anarchy, they might sooner recover their grandeurs and possessions. The whole history of the Revolution, from its alpha to its omega, from its first thought to its last deed, from Voltaire to Talleyrand, is written in the perfidy of nobles. [18]

I have . . . endeavoured to show, while the French Aristocracy was attired in her robes of state, and decked out with all those golden presents which the Bourbons delighted to lavish on her, that she was unsound, and rotten to the core. Brilliant as was her illustration, I have not been blind to her defects. [20] . . . But the Aristocracy of France is now presented to our view in a far different attitude and aspect. They have undergone a great and terrible vengeance. They have been doomed to a shameful and bitter penance. Emigration and Death with the Revolution, – Exile and Proscription with the Empire, – Slight and Disappointment with the Restoration, – Disqualification and Disgrace with the July dynasty! From the moment when their fathers rode out of Paris, with the flames still smouldering beneath the ruins of the Bastille, down to this our own time, their career has been one long mortification. The sternest of moralists will admit that the retribution has been more than ample. The severest of republicans might be moved at the recollection of some among its earlier passages. [21] . . .

. . . [At] the Restoration . . . it seemed as if the old things were to come back in the old ways. A Richelieu . . . was made Prime Minister . . . in virtue, it might appear, of his family's prescriptive right to rule beneath the Bourbons. The great charges were restored to their former holders, or to the families in which they had become inherent. . . . But these things were but the shadows of the past. They were the living semblance of a dead reality – a Mezentian attempt to yoke the departed and [**25**] the present, the spirit that had gone, and the form that was only permitted to exist. The fifteen years, which made the Restoration, were little less trying to the aristocracy, than had been their exile. Their estates were only partially restored. Their titles were usurped. The law of entails was not re-enacted. The old privileges were gone. The parliaments had passed away. The seigneural rights were never named, except for disavowal or abhorrence. Their juster claims were unheeded by the king. They were adjudicated upon by strange courts, which had grown up beneath a stranger code.[22]

But they bore up with fruitless gallantry against the tide. It was all in vain that they were more monarchical than the monarch, more Bourbon than the Bourbons. They opposed the misplaced concessions of Louis XVIII. They had no share in the misplaced resistance to Charles X. For this time the tragedy was to be travestied and reversed. It was not the aristocracy which destroyed the monarchy. It was the monarchy which destroyed the aristocracy. It almost reads like the first two plays of an Athenian trilogy, (the third of which is hereafter to be discovered,) so sustained was the gloomy reciprocity of Fate and Retribution.

Another fifteen years have now well nigh passed [**26**] away, and the clouds have not yet become dispersed. But let what may be, the vicissitudes of France, and the wisest among us, are unable to foretell them, the great names will always re-appear. This is no unreasoning or thoughtless theory. They are entrenched deep in the pride of the nation. Their strongholds are the vanities of the vainest of people. Even the most enthusiastic republicans will ostentatiously tell you that alone of all the ancient monarchies, France is still ruled by an indigenous Sovereign. Even the most fanatical of democrats will boast that alone in poverty and ruin his nobles receive a deference of which aristocracies far more flourishing are ignorant. [**27**] . . . Nor, what is not without account among a light people, are the materials deficient of a brilliant and fascinating court. . . . But all these elements of elegance and courtesy, all these appliances of polish and refinement, are [**28**] now neutralised by the alienation of the Faubourg from the Tuileries.[23]

There may be in this but little of political prudence. There cannot be much of self-denial and sincerity. The question which they have to determine is the most difficult which conscience can have to entertain. Let no one blame their decision. It is one which Great Publicists have affirmed with equal confidence on either side; – it is one which no casuist has been able to elucidate, – no divine been competent to certify. It is the old doubt between a love of order and a love of opinion; the old choice between the duty of obedience with peace, or the satisfaction of faith with disturbance. Who shall pronounce a judgement? Who shall weight the exact amount of truth and error, where there must inevitably be so much of both? Who can presume, in the vanity of his intellect, to blame the alternative, which the wisdom of all time has still left indeterminate? Who would not rather learn – when the right is thus doubtful and ambiguous – a lesson of forbearance and toleration?

For on the one hand it is a sad thing that men . . . whose sympathy is necessarily on the side of authority, should be compelled by the falseness of their position to weaken [29] and oppose it.[24] Is it not a melancholy thought that genius and eloquence such as theirs should be neutralized for effective good by their romantic allegiance and refined devotion to the past? How mournful is their political position! Absolutists, they are playing the game of democracy – conservatives they are promoting disturbance, – loyalists, they are leading to revolution. Is there right principle in this? Are not the principles irrespective of man's changes – of dynasties and persons – of kingdoms and their overthrow? . . . [T]heirs must be an irksome and ungrateful task for temperaments which are alive to all the beauty of order, but which are seeking to mar its fairness, – which carry with them convictions which every day they are obliged to belie – which feel all the force of that truth which every hour they are obliged to contradict. . . .

On the other hand, and notwithstanding all this falseness [30] of position, there is no such example in our times of that public virtue, which is so rare among communities, and which may suggest a comparison with Plataean self-devotion, – and perhaps for as ungrateful as Athens. Still, it is a touching and heroic spectacle. A race which remains apart, as it were, self-exiled in its own country – which prefers the faith of their fathers, before all things, – which clings to the elder line as to its visible presence, – which through penury, and shame, and insult, have never forsaken or abated an opinion. And they have had their reward. They are freed from splendid sins and great temptations. They have no longer a vulgar or immediate ambition. Their connection with the State – for Aristocracy has its own Erastianism to rue – is now no more. The golden shackles are removed. They are breathing the free air of their ancestral estates. They are mingling with the people. Out of abasement they have gained new powers. They have found new strength in the soil. They have derived new faculties, experiences, influences, requirements, from their robust and plain-spoken associates. And, if ever they shall again be called to govern, they will not forget the lessons of their allies, nor the sympathy which their own long knowledge of calamity must surely have provoked. [**31**]

But I am already more than presumptuous in attempting to praise or blame contemporaries. It is not given to a foreigner to discriminate between the nice shades of party difference, or even to adjudge between those nobles who affect Orleans Tuileries, or those who prefer the workshops of the people. It is sufficient that his own admiration is disinterested and sincere. He has ventured to pay the Aristocracy of France a homage full of regret for the past, full of solicitude for the future. It is offered in their misfortune and decline. His praise, however valueless, is not for the powerful; his song, however humble, not for the prosperous. And, in his augury of a fairer fortune, he hazards no political opinion if he has been unable to separate their destinies from those of the Elder Bourbons, with whom, all their renown, their virtues, their defects, and it may be their hopes, are connected. [**32**]

(iii)   *The Corruption of Aristocracy in England*

Benjamin Disraeli, *Sybil*[25]

Egremont was the younger brother of an English earl, whose nobility being of nearly three centuries' date, ranked him among our high and ancient peers, although its origin was more memorable than illustrious. The Founder of the family had been a confidential domestic of one of the favourites of Henry the Eighth, and had contrived to be appointed one of the commissioners for 'visiting and taking the surrenders of divers religious houses'. It came to pass that divers of these religious houses surrendered themselves eventually to the use and benefit of Baldwin Greymount. The king was touched with the activity and zeal of his commissioner. Greymount was noticed; sent for; promoted in the household; knighted; might doubtless have been sworn of the council, and in due time have become a minister; but his was a discreet ambition – of an accumulative rather than an aspiring character. He served the king faithfully in all domestic matters that required an unimpassioned, unscrupulous agent;

fashioned his creed and conscience according to the royal model in all its freaks; seized the right moment to get sundry grants of abbey lands, and contrived in that dangerous age to save both his head and his estate.

The Greymount family having planted themselves in the land, faithful to the policy of the founder, avoided the public gaze during the troubled period that followed the reformation; and even during the more orderly reign of Elizabeth, rather sought their increase in alliances than in court favour. But at the commencement of the seventeenth century, their abbey lands infinitely advanced in value, and their rental swollen by the prudent accumulation of more than seventy years, a Greymount . . . was elevated to the peerage as Baron Marney. The heralds furnished his pedigree, and assured the world that although the exalted rank and extensive possessions enjoyed at present by the Greymounts, had their origin immediately in great territorial revolutions of a recent reign, it was not for a moment to be supposed, that the remote ancestors of the Ecclesiastical Commissioner of 1530 were by any means obscure. On the contrary, it appeared that they were both Norman and baronial, their real name Egremont, which, in their patent of peerage the family now resumed.

In the civil wars, the Egremonts pricked by their Norman blood, were cavaliers and fought pretty well, but in 1688, alarmed at the prevalent impression that King James intended to insist on the restitution of the church estates to their original purposes, to wit, the education of the people and the maintenance of the poor, the Lord of Marney Abbey became a warm adherent to 'civil and religious liberty' . . . and joined the other whig lords, and great lay impropriators, in calling over the Prince of Orange and a Dutch army, to vindicate popular principles which, somehow or other, the people would never support. Profiting by this last pregnant circumstance, the lay Abbot of Marney also in this instance like the other whig lords, was careful to maintain, while he vindicated the cause of civil and religious liberty, a very loyal and dutiful though secret correspondence with the court of St Germains.[26]

The great deliverer King William the Third, to whom Lord Marney was a systematic traitor, made the descendant of the Ecclesiastical Commissioner of Henry the Eighth an English earl; and from that time until the period of our history, though the Marney family had never produced one individual eminent for civil or military abilities, though the country was not indebted to them for a single statesman, orator, successful warrior, great lawyer, learned divine, eminent author, illustrious man of science, they had contrived, if not to engross any great share of public admiration and love, at least to monopolise no contemptible portion of public money and public dignities. During the seventy years of almost unbroken whig rule, from the accession of the House of Hanover to the fall of Mr Fox, Marney Abbey had furnished a never-failing crop of lord privy seals, lord presidents, and lord lieutenants. The family had their due quota of garters and governors and bishoprics; admirals without fleets, and generals who fought only in America. They had glittered in great embassies with clever secretaries at their elbow, and had once governed Ireland when to govern Ireland was only to apportion the public plunder to a corrupt senate.

(iv)   *A Discordant Note from Outside Parliament*

[Anon.], 'Lord John Manners and the Manchester "Conservatives"'[27]

. . . Before Lord JOHN MANNERS can expect the country to sympathise with his heart wish respecting 'old Tory principles', he must define what these principles are; for despicable though the abstract something or nothing 'Conservatism' be, it is much more likely to captivate the affections of 'Young England' than the extinct system of tyranny and intolerance usually denominated Toryism.

4 Monarchy

Young England attempted to present an image of monarchy that would make it an appealing symbol of responsible hierarchy. In so doing, its members presented critiques of challenges to royal authority that had occurred in the last two centuries, and they also assigned blame to rulers who had besmirched the image of monarchy. The beginning of a new reign under a youthful queen provided the opportunity for England to break with an uninspiring tradition of monarchy that had been established since the Glorious Revolution of 1688.

(i) The Lessons of English and French History

Lord John Manners, 'England's Trust'[28]

IV

> . . .
> Trace the connexion that is clearly seen
> The natural parent and the State between,
> And see how evenly, when men began
> To slight the symbol, they unkinged the man. [31]
> Each year has loosened further still the ties
> Between divine and human sympathies,
> Till now, too liberal and enlightened grown,
> We laugh at all commandment, save our own.

Seems it not strange to our perverted view,
To read the terms of awe, which sons thought due
To sires, and which those sires thought due, again,
To all above them in the social chain!
Where now is that fond reverence, that spread
A halo round the regal head,
And showed the world a more than earthly thing –
The Lord's anointed in a sceptred king?
. . . [32]

George Smythe, 'Louis XIV and Charles II'[29]

The monarchies of Louis the Fourteenth, and Charles the Second, are the half-way house between Chivalry and Fashion. The faith of the first, with many of its old solemnities, was declining. The eclecticism of the last, in all its unreasoning exclusiveness, was beginning. It is a mean passage in the world's history. But there are many reasons why a Frenchman should refer to it with pride. To Englishmen it ought to seem the most shameful of our annals. And yet, it is strange, that it has always been a favourite. 'The Merry Monarch' has been the hero of more fictions, plays, and romances, than any other of our Kings. The greatest of our moralists, Dr. Johnson, was never tired of sounding his panegyric. The greatest of our novelists, Sir Walter Scott, has drawn his likeness in lineaments more flattering, – (where all that was harsh and repulsive has been [67] more skilfully softened) than in any portrait of Sir Peter Lely. The truth is, that Charles the Second was at best a sort of provisional Louis Quatorze. He ranted, upon a smaller stage, that part of 'Captain Absolute' which the other performed. His Buckinghams and Rochesters were coarse caricatures of the Villerois and the Rohans. His Wycherly was an execrable Moliere. His Cleveland was a tawdry Montespan. It was evident, from the disgust of the spectators, that the curtain would fall sooner in England than in France. It did so but four years after his death – to the ruin of his brother and successor.[30]

There is also this striking difference between England and France at the period to which I am alluding. They had a small Rebellion and a great Monarchy. We had a great Rebellion and a small monarchy. The vilest traits of personal littleness, such as Ashley's hypocrisy, and Orleans' treason, are to be found in the Cabal of Charles II, and in the Intrigues of the Fronde. The noblest examples of individual heroism, Hampden and Strafford, Fenelon and Bossuet, belong to our Parliamentary troubles, and to their Absolutist court.[31] . . . [**68**]

George Smythe, 'The Touching for the Evil'[32]

[. . .] Under King Charles the Second, the angel-gold, which was distributed by the King's almoners, to those who came to be touched, amounted to five thousand [pounds] a year. This was a large sum, to be given in immediate charity, when it is considered that the whole of the public revenue was under a million and a half. It was a thousand a year more than the combined salaries of the Secretaries of State, a thousand a year more than the allowance of Prince Rupert. But it is not so much the amount, which makes a regret for this graceful superstition, as the direct communication it brought about, between the highest and the lowest, between the King and the Poor. If Royalty did but descend to lower itself to a familiarity with the [**91**] people, it is curious that they will raise, exalt, adore it, sometimes even invest it with divine and mysterious attributes; if, on the contrary, it shuts itself up in an august and solemn seclusion, it will be mocked and caricatured. This was one of the secrets of Napoleon's strength, and one of the secrets of Louis XVIIIth's weakness. If the great only knew what stress the poor lay by the few forms which remain to join them, they would make many sacrifices for their maintenance and preservation. Dr. Johnson – a man of the people if ever there was one, – was yet prouder of having been touched by Queen Anne, when he was a child, of speaking about 'the great lady in black,' of whom he had an indistinct recollection, than he was of all his heroism under misfortune, or of all the erudition of his works.[33] [**92**]

George Smythe, 'King James the Second'[34]

When King James the Second was for the last time in London, he was received with shouts of welcome, and cheers of affection by the population. It was a great lesson, which it was too late for the Royal hearer to profit by. But if there did not glance across his mind the secret of that, which ought to have been his strength, he could not have been without a suspicion of the secret of his weakness. Where were all those silken courtiers, whom the lavish favour of his house had so fostered and caressed? Where were all those insolent nobles, whom the Charles's had raised with such wanton prodigality, out of meanness and obscurity? Where was all that debauched Aristocracy, the gay guests of Hampton Court, the betters of Newmarket and the basset table, the compliant husbands, the officious panders, for whom place on place, and pension on pension, had been created, for whom England had not gold enough, – minions and hirelings of France, – whose [93] ostentatious excesses had done more than any Embassy to Rome, to animate the Puritan, and alienate the Protestant? Who were they? History informs us, – but it is in the list of honours of the dynasty succeeding. Oh when will the rulers of the earth understand that their natural allies are the Many, their natural enemies the privileged and the Few!

The grandson of the Clarendon, who had been so enriched by the Stuarts, was the first to go over, with three regiments to the Invader. The Danby who had been the Minister of Charles the Second, was to become the first Duke of the new Dynasty. The Churchill, who owed his peerage to his sister's favour, was to be its Hero. The House of Townsend, which derived its nobility from the Restoration, – was to become the great nursery of Ministers for the Constitutional Monarchy, which replaced it.[35]

[. . .] King James, was thus the victim of a policy for which he was not responsible. The great nobles, the Sunderlands, Danbys, Halifaxes, who betrayed him, had been already elevated by others to that station, from which it was impossible for him to remove them.[36] It was in vain for him to look for support from the Church of England. His design [94] (to any one who will consult his autobiography, this will be clear) was not so much to establish Roman Catholicism as to reconcile the Churches. Vain dream! In our time it might stimulate the hopes and sympathies of some enthusiasts; – in his, it excited universal alienation. And when the Church raised that cry, which has since proved fatal to so many ministries, and which was then powerful [enough] to destroy a Monarchy, 'The Church is in danger,' the House of Stuart, opposed by the clergy, and betrayed by the aristocracy, ceased to reign. It has given to History, in the fall of King James, and the exile of his descendants, the most romantic of misfortunes, but there will always be more of general sympathy for that ruler who conspired *with* his people, *against* his nobles.

It might be a curious speculation what would have been the fate of James the Second, if he had profited by his grandfather's example in France, if like him he had changed his religion, if he had joined the League of Augsbourg, if he had abandoned the alliance of Louis XIV. . . .[37] It is perhaps an idle task thus to mar the symmetry [95] of the past, and disturb the harmony of

Providence. But it was impossible not to give way to some such reflections, while we stood, on a bright July day, in the little Church of St. Germains. Mass was saying for the soul of the Duke of Orleans. The nave was full of soldiers, who were upon duty for the melancholy ceremony. Before us was the tomb of James the Second. How mournful a renewal of old times, was there, in those two names of Orleans and Stuart! It brought back the tradition of that superb and festive marriage, between Orleans and Stuart, between the brother of Louis XIV., and the loveliest woman of her time, Henrietta of England, who inherited all the beauty of her father, who was so admired at the Court of France, who was so loved by the young and brilliant de Guiche, who died so sad a death, but whose memory is immortalized in the noblest of modern eloquence, the oration of Bossuet on her death.[38]

But there was another association of names close by us, scarcely less suggestive of thought. It was the inscription which King George the Fourth had caused to be put upon the monument which he had raised to King James the Second – the homage of a Constitutional Monarch to the last Absolute King of England. [**96**]

Lord John Manners, 'King Charles the Martyr'[39]

> Thou monarch-martyr! fain would I
> In meet expressions own
> Thy boundless sovereignty,
> Thou captive on a throne,
> O'er my soul's pulses; but in vain
> The attempt, too grand, I make.
> My feeble-hearted strain
> Trembles to undertake
> A theme so sacred, yet I feel
> The memories of thy fate
> Cut through my heart as steel,
> Prompting to emulate
> Thy high resolve and steadfast faith,
> That knew not how to cower,
> That triumphed over death,
> And blessed thee in that hour
> Of sin, and sorrow, and unhallowed power! [**65**]

(ii)   *The Young Queen*

Benjamin Disraeli, *Sybil*[40]

[Peel] ought to have taken office in 1839. His withdrawal seems to have been a mistake. In the great heat of parliamentary faction which had prevailed since 1831, the royal prerogative, which, unfortunately, for the rights and liberties and social welfare of the people, had since 1688 been more or less oppressed, had waned fainter and fainter. A youthful princess on the throne, whose appearance touched the imagination, and to whom her people were generally inclined to ascribe something of that decision of character which becomes those born to command, offered a favourable opportunity to restore the exercise of the regal authority, the usurpation of whose functions had entailed on the people of England so much suffering and so much degradation.

George Smythe, Speech to the Electors of Canterbury, 8 January 1841[41]

It is now two hundred years since . . . our great party . . . sprung full-armed into life, to rally round the monarchy, and protect it from insult. Then, when it was falling, my ancestors rallied around it too . . . . They suffered fine and confiscation, at a time when justice was administered by the sword of Cromwell, and when the muster roll of his favourite regiment of 'Ironsides' availed more than the *Magna Charta* . . . . But I will say more – that I do not want those reasons for being loyal. I am loyal, not to the institution only, but to the person. If I see one more gentle than Anne – more courageous than Elizabeth – more graceful and winning than Mary Stuart – more earnest and constant in her attachment than Mary Tudor, – a Queen with all those Queens' virtues, and none of their defects, surely she should be popular . . . . I feel it is what she ought to be, and if she is not so, it is the fault of her weak government. Now, what we want is a strong government, and I am sure that you feel so too. With a strong government, and with such a Queen as we have, we could not fail to be foremost among nations.

5   The Role of Commerce

Although they were strongly attached to ideas of traditional order, Young England writers did not set their faces completely against commercial society. To the contrary, both Manners and Smythe thought that commerce would produce significant non-material benefits if its dehumanizing and destabilizing tendencies could be kept in check. Manners was thus sympathetic to the cultural and intellectual aspirations of the urban middle classes, and Smythe looked forward to a free and glorious future for literature that would parallel that produced by free trade. He also saw romance and grandeur in the achievements of merchant princes: they added a new dimension to the expression of these values in aristocratic life.

(i)   *Commerce and Middle-Class Culture*

Lord John Manners, Speech at the Opening of the Manchester Athenaeum Institute[42]

Ladies, Mr Chairman, and Gentleman,
I will frankly own to you that when I first received the flattering invitation to attend this most splendid and interesting assemblage, I almost hesitated as to whether I should accept it or not, because I could not help feeling that a stranger, from another part of the country, might perhaps be almost out of his place in coming forward to take a part in a concern wholly affecting the interests of this great hive of manufacturing industry; but then I recollected that Manchester

'Young Manchester'. *Punch*'s view of youthful chivalry in the machine age.

(*From the Alexander Turnbull Library, National Library of New Zealand,
Te Puna Mātauranga o Aotearoa*, ref no. S-L 190.)

had now, by the skill, and industry, and perseverance, of her children, become
intimately and inseparably a portion of the whole of this mighty kingdom, and
that therefore every Englishman might fairly claim a share in her exertions to
promote the best interests of her sons, might sympathise in her endeavours to
exalt the condition of her people, and might share in her splendid hospitality. . . . It is indeed, to anyone who remembers that the name of Englishmen
ought to be a name of far greater import, and possessing a far more potent
spell, than either Whig or Tory, a subject of most sincere congratulation to find
a field whereon politicians of all shades of opinion may meet without fear of
quarrelling. – . . . Still more would I hope that the meeting may produce a result
which may increase the means of providing intellectual and innocent
amusement for the great middle classes of this metropolis. . . .

The . . . reason why so many mechanics' institutions were opposed at their
commencement, and since that commencement have languished, and many of

them have fallen, was that deserting and perhaps exceeding their natural and legitimate province, they arrogated for themselves, or, at least, their advocates arrogated for them, the education of the youth of this country; and I confess, that when I heard the other day at Birmingham, a young artisan explaining the causes of the decadence of all such institutions in his own town, I could not but be struck with his assertion, that the reason why they had fallen was, that they had forgotten amusement in instruction . . . and were acting upon the untenable principle that a man, after a long and laborious day's work, could sit down to recreate his mind with a course of astronomy, or a series of lectures on geology, – that such a system as that could properly be called recreation and amusement for the people. If, therefore, ladies and gentlemen, I had heard that the Manchester Athenaeum was founded on a basis of that sort, I confess I should have hesitated to present myself before you this evening . . . but, believing as I do, that your Athenaeum professes to provide intellectual and literary amusement and recreation for those already educated, to mould, to soften, and to elevate the tastes of the great middle classes of the community, and to encourage literature and rising art, I have the greatest pleasure in coming forward to express my cordial sympathy in those endeavours, and my humble but hearty meed of commendation of those aims and objects . . . .

[. . .] In the meeting of this morning I could not also help being struck with the facts which the various deputations from the various towns of Lancashire brought forward, respecting the tastes of the readers belonging to those institutions. There was one fact which I cannot help reverting to: it was the most gratifying announcement, that the study of history was one which was most peculiarly acceptable in those institutions; . . . and it is a matter to me of no small congratulation to think, that, commensurate with this increased partiality to history, do we find a new spirit infused into the writing of history, and that we see a spirit of truth – seeking inquisition abroad, which will not rest contented with the low and party views of historians of the last century – but which will investigate and search out the *data* on which all history ought to be formed, and present it as it really is, and not as the writers of it may wish it to be.[43] And, ladies and gentlemen, permit me to say, that it is to associations like this, and to meetings like the present, that they who are opening, as I believe, the way to a better and more just appreciation of the past, must look for support and encouragement against that opposition and obloquy, which they who disturb the slumbers of contented lethargy must always encounter. . . .

And, proceeding to another department, – one to which I attach peculiar importance – the department of the fine arts and of taste, – I think no one will now deny that a most marked improvement has taken place in the popular mind in that respect, even within the memory of the youngest of us here present. . . . Glance over the advertisements in the papers; look at the works which lie on the counter of every bookseller's shop in the towns; as you travel by the rail-road, look at the works on the stalls of the various stations; listen to the lectures delivered by such men as Professors Willis and Dyce; and we must all acknowledge that a marked improvement has taken place in the popular mind with respect to the fine arts and matters of taste. . . . Christian art . . . is once more raising its head in this and other countries, and bids fair, not perhaps to surpass, but to emulate its pristine splendour and beauty.[44]

Be it yours, then, – be it part of the Manchester Athenaeum, – to encourage and to foster that reviving literature, and that struggling art. Be it yours to remove the reproach which, I trust, now has become obsolete, – that manufactures must produce a dry, unpoetical, and material spirit. Be it yours to refute the terrible contrast which has been drawn by the master architect of the day between a supposed Manchester of 1480 and a real Manchester of 1840.[45] Be it yours to soften and to elevate the tastes of those by whose exertions the wealth of this great metropolis has been made. And beyond all this, do I know well enough, that there remains a still higher and a still more difficult task to perform. But do this and you will have done a great somewhat; and believe me that your children's children will bless those evenings which were spent as this evening is being spent, in good fellowship, in the interchange of sympathies, and of kind wishes between the various classes of the community, and in an endeavour, – I trust it may be a successful one, – to soften the harsh tendencies of toil and wealth, by the gentle influences of literature and the fine arts.

(ii)   Commerce and Literature

George Smythe, Speech at the Opening of the Manchester Athenaeum Institute[46]

. . . I will venture to predict for the literature that shall result from such a meeting as the present, that shall derive its impulse from such a spirit, that shall be fostered and encouraged by such sympathies as yours, a destiny yet more lasting and auspicious; because it will not . . . lean upon the need for patronage; it will not be patronised by monarchs; it will not be fashioned by nobles. It shall be free, independent, universal, and tolerant commerce. (Massive applause)

. . . It is impossible for any one to have studied the history of the last half-century, without perceiving that Manchester has always been foremost in the great work of national advancement. I have said before, you represent a great necessity; I believe there is a great work to do, and I believe that *you* will do it. It seems to me that you, who have already carried your material triumphs to the remotest corners of the earth, have also remembered that there was still another world to conquer. Nor will your triumphs in this spiritual world be less remarkable, because that same creative power, which in the world of action is called invention, and which aids, and serves, and ministers to man, – that same creative power, in the world of thought is called genius, and governs and provides for man. But in either sphere, be it of thought or of action, your object is ever the same: it is your high and holy mission to benefit mankind. There is nothing small, there is nothing exclusive, there is nothing partial, there is nothing . . . sectarian in the spirit of British commerce. It was out of a temper as catholic and universal, that the humanities first sprang; it will be out of a temper as catholic that here, in the metropolis of English enterprise, great things will be done.

(iii) *Commerce and National Grandeur*

George Smythe, 'The Merchants of Old England'[47]

III

The land it boasts its titled hosts – they cannot vie with these,
The Merchants of old England – the Seigneurs of the Seas,
In the days of Queen Victoria, for they have borne her sway
From the far Atlantic islands, to the islands of Cathay,
And, o'er one-sixth of all the earth, and over all the main,
Like some good Fairy, Freedom marks and blesses her domain.
And of the mighty empires, that arose, and ruled, and died,
Since on the sea, his heritage, the Tyrian ruled in pride,
Not Carthage, with her Hannibal, not Athens when she bore
Her bravest and her boldest to the Syracusan shore,
While the words of Alcibiades yet echoed wide and far,

'Where are corn fields, and are olive grounds, the Athenian's limits are.'
And in each trireme was many a dream of the West, and its un-known bliss
Of the maidens of Iberia, and the feasts of Sybaris –
Not in those younger ages, when St. Mark's fair city ran
Her race of fame and frailty, – each monarch's courtezan,
Not Lusia in her palmier hour, in those commercial days,
When Vasco sailed for Calicut, and Camöens sang his praise, [385]
Not Spain with all her Indies, the while she seemed to fling,
Her fetters on the waters, like the oriental king,
Not one among the conquerors that are or ever were,
In wealth, or fame, or grandeur with England may compare.
But not of this our Sovereign thought, when from her solemn throne,
She spoke of the Poor, and what they endure, in her low and Thrilling tone,
And offered a prayer that Trade might bear relief through the starving land,
To the strong man's weakened arm, and his wan and workless hand,
And by the power, that was her dower, might Commerce once more be
That Helper of the Helpless, and the Saviour of the Free.
Then Glory to the Merchants, who shall do such deeds as these,
The Merchants of Old England, the Seigneurs of the Seas. [386]

6 Political Practice

Both within Parliament and in the country, Young England was critical of the ethos and practice of modern party government. The movement presented itself as guardian of national interests that cut across class, party and sect. It was claimed that modern parties were not attached to coherent principles, relying instead on thinly veiled self-interest, opportunism, or the promotion of a cult of administrative expertise. The revival of an authentic aristocratic spirit in politics was seen as a way of correcting these tendencies. If this strategy was to be effective, however, aristocratic politicians would have to learn to take account of national interests and to adapt their practice to the requirements of modern politics. Smythe was particularly interested in the requirements of effective leadership.

(i) The Malign Spirit of Party in Modern Politics

[Anon.], 'Present Condition of Political Parties'[48]

On the eve of the meeting of Parliament, the present condition of parties is a question full of interest and anxiety to the nation at large. The time has gone by when this was merely a topic of clubs, or of aristocratic society. In those days two notes only made themselves heard. The 'ins' shouted their song of triumph; the 'outs' replied with a growl of defiance. At present – in the year of grace 1845 – a third voice, more powerful than either, the intelligent voice of the nation, decides who shall be the 'ins', and what shall be the tenure of office.

And here, lest we be misunderstood, – here, once for all, we declare, that by the voice of the nation we do not covertly intend the discordant shout of the masses, – of mere numbers, irrespective of all those accidents and qualities which invest opinion with authority: frankly, we intend the intelligence and education of the nation, moulded by habits of thought, and chastened by the influence of religion. Such is, in fact, that element in a state – place it in what class or number of classes you may – which, after all, acts upon its points of contact with irresistible energy and power; saps the sandy foundations of false and vicious theories; and, by its intrinsic weight, ever preserves the balance of a state wherein it exists, in times even of social convulsion, when mere government is paralysed, and the law in abeyance.

[. . .] At the close of the last session it was a common remark, even in the mouth of the oldest political hack, that parties, as such, existed no more. It was impossible to guess on mere party ground which way any given man of eminence would vote. . . . Upon a general glance at Parliament, the feature presented itself of a certain tameness and reserve even in ministerial deportment, as if the whole session were but an interlude, and the strength of the performers were husbanded for some important subsequent representation.

On a nearer view it was perceived that Conservatism had degenerated into Peelism; that the principle, if any such there was, of that influential party was scattered to the winds, and that they were content to vote white today and black tomorrow, at the stern bidding of their NEMESIS. Unlucky Conservatives! Who does not remember the old nursery tales of the Gentleman in Black, and his amiable forbearance up to a certain point? When *that* is reached, comes the fatal bond; and the soul of Conservatism (which we presume is its honour) is claimed as a forfeit, and after many a hard struggle is delivered up to the no longer obsequious fiend.

Yet before we part with 'Conservatism', let us be just to its merits. But for this amiable watchword, this sonorous property-cry, beyond question we had been in a far worse condition than we now are. The Ministry of Conservatism has paid our debts, and put us in the way of keeping straight for some time to come. Thus, if no large principle be enunciated, no deep-searching policy applied to the *vexata questio* of the day – the condition of the lower classes – the nation is yet in a favourable position to look into the matter for itself; as a man at ease in his domestic circumstances can apply his energies and his talents unfettered to the solution of questions which an embarrassed man must resign in despair.

Of the Whigs, as a party, it is a loss of time to speak. Pure unadulterated Whiggism may possibly survive, as a graceful souvenir, in certain boudoirs and salons where symbols heroically outlive the things symbolised. As a reality, that once respectable party is extinct. Overtaken by Conservatism in front, pressed and trampled upon by [57] Radicalism in the rear, the main body of the Whigs are worn down to nothing between the two advancing forces. It must never be forgotten that this catastrophe is solely attributable to themselves. From whatever cause, their decennial period of office was used by them, as if advisedly, to destroy and annihilate the prestige that hailed the first Reformers in power. Large conceders in name, in reality granting no solid boon to the nation, timid in action, juggling in parliamentary tactics, they earned and deserved the contempt of all parties. . . .

There remains the (so-called) Radical party, professing intelligible views, putting forward certain broad principles. Could this party only convince each other of their mutual honesty, what great things, whether for good or evil, might not be achieved by men who *profess* exclusively the rights of the lower orders. But it seems fated that mankind should distrust these aspiring moralists; nor was it, probably, without a view to these pinnacle-seeking philosophists, that Satan is represented to have chosen for the seat of his last temptation the highest point of the temple.

In fact, the leading Radicals most thoroughly distrust each other, and the hobbies they severally ride are so trained as to justify more than a slight suspicion of the real purposes of the riders. They prance and amble, and run tilts with ministers at given signals, and on preconcerted field-days. That the courses are run with blunted lances; the jester, embodied in some facetious ultra-ist on one side or both, carries off the real honours of the day, and combatants separate, out of breath, indeed, but sound in life and limb, and ready to renew the mock contest as soon as it is thought convenient to throw the sawdust of this bloodless arena in the eyes of complacent constituents.

From such elements it is hopeless to seek the cohesion and the oneness – not to say the truth and honesty – of a great party. There are in the Radical ranks many men of undoubted power and energy, many men of political talent, not a few of singleness of purpose and well-defined views. But as a party they fail, and for this reason: full of salient points as they are, their composition is of wood, not of firm granite. The former material requires apt fitting to make it whole; it is only the latter more enduring substance that amalgamates by attrition and owes its cohesion to its opposing angles.

The result of our brief summary of parties in the House of Commons is favourable to the view of the small but increasing section known under the name which this journal has adopted; adopted, however, for itself, and without being bound to the opinions of any men whatever. Taking, however, those views in the most general sense, as earnest and hearty aspirations after a healthier state of things among the productive classes, irrespective of party, we say, *now is the time* when they must make their way, if practically brought forward. The sympathy of the nation is with them, and if ever the *vox populi* deserved its ambitious antitheses, it is surely now, when uplifted on behalf of unparalleled distress patiently suffering side by side with unexampled prosperity. . . . **[58]**

Benjamin Disraeli, *Coningsby*[49]

The Tamworth Manifesto of 1834[50] was an attempt to construct a party without principles; its basis was necessarily latitudinarianism; and its inevitable consequence has been political infidelity. . . .

There was indeed a considerable shouting about what they called Conservative principles; but the awkward question naturally arose, what will you conserve? The prerogatives of the crown, provided they are not exercised; the independence of the House of Lords, provided it is not asserted; the ecclesiastical estate, provided it is regulated by a commission of laymen. Everything in short that is established, as long as it is a phrase and not a fact. . . .

Conservatism was an attempt to carry on affairs by substituting the fulfilment of the duties of office for the performance of the functions of government; and to maintain this negative system by the mere influence of property, reputable private conduct, and what are called good connections. Conservatism discards Prescription, shrinks from Principle, disavows Progress; having rejected all respect for Antiquity, it offers no redress for the Present, and makes no preparation for the Future. It is obvious that for a time, under favourable circumstances, such a confederation might succeed; but it is equally clear, that on the arrival of one of those critical conjunctures that will periodically occur in all states, and which such an unimpassioned system is even calculated ultimately to create, all power of resistance will be wanting; the barren curse of political infidelity will paralyse all action; and the Conservative constitution will be discovered to be a caput mortuum.

(ii) *Aristocracy and Modern Politics*

Lord John Manners, 'The Corn Laws and the Aristocracy'[51]

I

Let us not deceive ourselves: the country is in a great crisis: not one of those agreeably agitating conjunctures, when red tape officials tremble for their places, and the waiters upon Providence are in doubt whither to direct their interested devotions: but a crisis that may decide not only the future industrial policy of England, but the fate of its peerage, and form of its constitution. We cannot, entertaining such a conviction, shrink from reconsidering our judgement, and offering our advice to those, whose conduct mainly interests us at present – the territorial aristocracy of the country. With pseudo-Conservative statesmen, Free-trade orators, Whig converts, we have now nothing to do; but for the course pursued by the natural leaders of the people that it should be worthy of them, and equal to this grave emergency, we are painfully anxious. Solemn deliberation, to be followed it may be by bold and energetic action, is their first and paramount duty. Nothing, we know, is easier, nothing more grateful in some ways, to the feelings of high-couraged men, than on such an occasion as this to stop ears and eyes, and shouting 'No surrender,' rush blindly on to victory – or defeat. Such a course extracts but little painful thought, demands no anxious deliberation; would that it were sanctioned by true honour, wisdom, or patriotism! But no, we call upon the aristocracy to resist the temptation, and to apply all their energies to the solution of the terrible problem submitted to them. . . . [**82**]

. . . [W]hether owing to a misplaced confidence in the Government, or an equally misplaced want of confidence in themselves, the great agricultural party took no steps to meet the great and growing danger that was threatening them, until it had assumed a magnitude and power that rendered a protracted and fearful struggle certain, an ultimate conquest over it, to say the least, doubtful. And when the counter agitation was commenced, and the enlistment of the sympathies and support of the working classes throughout the country became as desirable as it was practicable, a selfish fear paralyzed the leaders of the agriculturists, and the Ten-hours' Bill was rejected to maintain the Corn Laws.[52] Shortsighted and wretched policy! The Ten-hours' Bill granted to the operatives of the North by the agriculturists of England, would have encircled the laws protective of English industry with a support and defence far more potent than that of ministers or societies – the affections of a long-enduring and grateful people.

But that golden opportunity was allowed to slip by: the word [**84**] of Peel prevailed more with the gentlemen of England than the prayers of their lowly fellow-countrymen, and now we read of the Preston operatives unanimously asking for a repeal of the Corn Laws, while the *Morning Post*, the only journal which with equal ability and consistency has advocated a highly protective policy, feels it right to assert that the present system of protection to agriculture is defective and inefficient, and must, in order to its just maintenance, be enlarged so as to cover the whole surface of English industry: such, too, is the opinion of many wise and patriotic men of eminence in our periodical literature. Is there, however, among the Protection Party generally, any desire thus to carry out their grand principle, or does the cry of 'Protection to English Industry' mean, in nine cases out of ten, anything more than a retention of the present sliding-scale? . . . We do not say that this is wrong . . . but we assert that the fact being so, places the Corn laws on an eminence, as it were, exposed to the darts of an infuriated enemy, and unguarded and undefended by the other numerous smaller protective duties that heretofore were auxiliary to them. This, we think, is a very important consideration, and one that should not be lost sight of by the leaders of the aristocracy at this crisis. If the Dukes of Richmond and Buckingham . . . were determined to carry on the struggle, we must submit to them that they should widen the base of the Protection Society, so as to comprise the hand-loom weavers of Lancashire, the framework-knitters of the midland counties, and all who live by English industry, in one great national league . . . . [**85**] If, however, the reverse is the fact, and the thousands whom live by the other branches of English industry cannot be won back again to the standard of protection, then let our leaders carefully review our present position, reckon their forces, count up the certain cost of the struggle, and estimate its possible result.

Nor let them be deterred from doing this their duty by the charge of cowardice, or the taunt of indecision. It is one thing for a garrison, ably officered, well provisioned, and plentifully supplied with all the munitions and resources of war, to surrender at the first hostile summons; and altogether another, for that garrison, deserted by its officers, with crippled means, and undermined walls, to enter into terms, and effect an honourable capitulation. The conduct we might blamelessly and wisely pursue in 1841, may now be far from wise and right. . . . [**86**]

[. . .] We do not say . . . the struggle . . . may not even ultimately end in the triumph of the land; but what must the cost and what the effects of such a triumph be? A protracted moral, if not physical, civil war, during which all confidence must be destroyed, the land relapsing into bad cultivation, or absolute barrenness, trade and agriculture both paralyzed, and each reacting unfavourably on the other, . . . and all the benefit the Corn Laws were intended to procure, steadiness of price, and security, absolutely lost . . . . [**87**]

Let us now . . . place in conclusion before our readers the courses it is open for that still powerful though partially broken party to pursue. First, they may abandon at once, and altogether the struggle, and adopting frankly and boldly their new position, with all its dangers, duties and responsibilities, offer the Corn Laws as a peace-offering to the genius of their country, and thus prove to the world alike the disinterestedness of their past resistance, and the magnanimity and courage of their present assent. . . . Great dangers require great ventures, and the moral effect of the gentlemen of England coming forward, and doing of themselves what neither Russell, nor Peel, nor Cobden could do without them, could not fail to be immense and salutary. But this step, if taken, must be taken with unblanched cheek and gallant bearing. It is the brave venture of men who, uncompelled, for their country's sake, leap, Curtius-like, into the gulf: there must be no murmuring, no complaining, no voting against the first reading of a bill, staying away on the second, and voting for the third: no unnecessary abuse of the others, no petulant attempts to render the sacrifice, if it be one, as little gracious as may be. If carried out in this magnanimous spirit, the aristocracy and gentlemen [**88**] of England may rely on their resolve being appreciated by the people. . . .

The second course that the agriculturalists may take, is that which a year ago Lord Grey, with all his impressive eloquence, urged upon them – a low fixed duty compromise. Then it was feasible; is it so now? . . . It is the old story over again – claims entirely rejected until they are entirely conceded: and such we believe to be a very general belief among the farmers; they see that such a compromise would afford no security to them . . . . [**89**] Speaking, however, without reference to the chances of success, we will say that *could* a fixed duty of 5*s* be maintained for ten or even five years longer, the perils attending a repeal of the Corn Laws would be greatly diminished, and the agricultural classes generally would be enabled to see their way through the mists of doubt and panic that now oppress them, to an intelligent and successful adaptation of their resources to their new position: while the march of agricultural improvement would be hastened rather than impeded by the anticipated change. But for the reasons above stated, we cannot think that this course is to be adopted with any success, and therefore dismiss the consideration of it to arrive at the remaining alternative, which enlists many of our sympathies and some little of our reason on its side, and is the obvious one for the country party, without deliberation, to adopt.

Should the aristocracy call upon the yeomanry and the rural population at large to maintain at all risks, and through all possible convulsions, the present Corn Laws, and govern the country on that basis? For this we apprehend to be the true statement of this alternative. A simply obstructive maintenance of the Corn Laws is no longer possible: it must be active, administrative. To turn one administration out after another, and not to find an efficient substitute for it, is not patriotism, but faction . . . . [T]he country party . . . must be prepared to step into the vacant seat of the stricken Phaeton, and conduct the car of government through all the dangers and obstacles of the way. . . .

We have already pointed to some of the disasters which we deem well nigh inevitable from a further protraction of the contest; let us now for a few moments consider the prospects of an administration pledged to maintain the present protection. . . . Such an administration, powerful from the position, habits of business, and talents [90] of its members, might, we well know, be formed tomorrow . . . . Nor is it to be doubted that they would, if violently assailed, be also enthusiastically supported; many mistakes, many short-comings would be overlooked in them, which in 'Sir Robert,' (who enjoys in the counties the favour and reputation which Sir Robert Walpole did during the last years of his rule,) would be freely commented upon . . . .

But short of this consumption, we repeat, opposition to Free Trade cannot stop, if intended *bona fide*. Mr. Christopher, nor Mr Miles, can never again look to Sir Robert Peel or Sir James Graham to reply to Mr. Villiers or Mr. Cobden.[53] They must trust to the independent country party alone for arguments and for votes. The whole *personnel* of the present Government is severed for ever from them . . . . [T]heir own energy, their own courage, their own eloquence, their own statesmanship, must conduct them through the storm; and if all these should fail, after a few years, [91] to win for them the victory, a recollection of the odds that were against them, and a consciousness of having done their duty according to their convictions, may console them in defeat. But once again must we implore their leaders to review with all impartiality and care the certain concomitants and probable results of adopting this last alternative.

We have thus, to the best of our ability, and with an honest endeavour to represent faithfully the political prospects with which the agricultural new year opens, presumed to offer these remarks to the consideration of the agricultural leaders. If they seem to be written in too desponding a spirit, and to recommend too yielding a line of conduct, it is because, on the one hand, we are oppressed by the saddest forebodings of the evil results that must follow the impending internecine contest; and on the other, have too great a confidence in English energy, English skill, English soil, and English climate, to look with equal dread at a competition with foreign farmers. We see little to be gained by a repeal of the Corn Laws, we see much to be hazarded by their retention; and under this impression, as junior officers at a council of war, we have ventured to speak our opinion, in no spirit of presumption, or fancied superior clearness of view beyond our elders and betters, but with an anxious desire of uniting once more the rapidly dissolving elements of English society, and combining in one league of loyalty and love under our youthful Queen, the peer and the millowner, the peasant and the manufacturing operative. . . . [**92**]

II

As we anticipated, the advice we presumed to offer in our last number to the leaders of the country party has not been followed, and, as is usual in such cases, the givers of it have been plentifully abused. A month has gone by, Parliament has met, the minister has announced his plan, the country party has denounced it, the fight has commenced, and we are more than ever, and most painfully, convinced of the soundness of that rejected advice. . . . Personal honour, a sense of indignation at the unworthy conduct of the minister, recollections of the past, anticipations of the future, and a natural disinclination to ally themselves with a cabinet, the [**191**] tool of a versatile though despotic minister, will doubtless prevent many English country gentlemen from supporting the ministerial measure. Nor in spite of our earnest conviction that in the right way, and at the right time, the Aristocracy should repeal the Corn Laws, can we wonder at, or blame this present resistance? The minister has consulted neither the private honour of his colleagues and party, nor the eventual public good of the country; and it is fitting and right that a protest should be made against conduct so humiliating now, and so fatal hereafter. Let us, however, while condemning the mode by which Sir Robert Peel is seeking to carry his changed convictions into practice, vindicate his full right to those convictions, lest we should for a moment seem to countenance the mad idea that a minister, entrusted with the government of a mighty people, is bound to sacrifice what reason and experience teach him is their truest good, to that wretched idol – party consistency. But in the application of this just theory of ministerial freedom to practice, there are conditions to be fulfilled, rules to be observed, decencies respected, feeling to be consulted, nay, if you will, even prejudices to be considered, if a great change, right and happy in itself, is to be permanently beneficial to the country; otherwise, the greatest material good may be accompanied by moral and social disadvantage, so grave and lasting as to not only counterbalance that good, but positively change the blessing into a curse. ... [**192**] Let this House of Commons, at the dictation of the Minister, repeal the Corn Laws, and let the House of Peers register that edict, and in an age of democratic tendencies, and waning authorities, the last ties of reverence and confidence between the rural middle, and lower, and upper classes are gone; nor they only, the belief in the consistency, and honour and high-mindedness of public men, is gone too; and throughout that great portion of the English community, that hitherto has opposed a traditional barrier against democracy and lawlessness, is spread a blank disbelief in coronets and cabinet ministers, aristocracies and hierarchies, which the steadiest trade in corn, and the happiest commercial intercourse with America, will not be able to dispel.

There never was a time, when the purest honour and most chivalrous scrupulousness were more demanded in public men than the present, for never had the State edifice fewer props to support it than now. The debauched aristocracy that ruled an ignorant and sparse population from the Revolution of 1688, to the close of the last century, might with impunity disregard public character, and forfeit all claims to consistency; the intelligence that alone could detect and punish such conduct, was itself equally guilty, and the spirits of Democracy and Atheism slumbered torpid in the whited sepulchres of dominant aristocracy and courtly scepticism. But now what stands there ... between order and revolution, but the popular belief in the integrity of great Statesmen, and the old bonds of sympathy and reverential regard between the various classes of rural England? and will not these two barriers be dashed down by Sir Robert Peel's unwisdom? ... [**194**]

... [B]eing persuaded that a great change in the Corn Laws would confer greater blessings on the country, than it would inflict evils, and consequently objecting not to the policy itself of the minister, but to the *when* and *to whom* it is proposed, we do not feel it necessary to comment on the various parts of his comprehensive and statesmanlike scheme. The handling of the Law of Settlement is Mr. Pitt's, and well indeed would it have been for the country if Sir Robert Peel, instead of sanctioning the Whig Poor Law of 1834, had proposed . . . that great statesman's whole measure of 1796, 'for the Employment, Instruction, and Relief of the Poor;' – but to throw the whole surface of English land open to English industry with a certainty that wherever labour has toiled, there shall it be supported, is a great, a noble, and a famous deed.[54] . . . Had we any hope of being listened to in the storm that is now blowing over the whole surface of English [**196**] society, we would gladly urge on the combatants now in presence, such an adjustment of their quarrel, but as it is, we can but retire from the now useless position of mediator, in the hope, and with the prayer, that after Englishmen have discovered how difficult it is to conquer Englishmen, they will remember that they are brethren, and each consent to sacrifice somewhat on the shattered altar of their common country. [**197**]

(iii) Political Leadership

George Smythe, 'Earl Grey'[55]

. . . [W]e shall, we hope, not be unjust in an attempt to give some slight idea of the great man, with whom, whether for good or evil, the Whig system has been for fifty years connected, by whose services it has been illustrated, by whose eloquence it has been vindicated, by whose consistency it has been maintained, by whose character it has been adorned, by whose existence alone it can be said of late years to have existed. [**196**] . . .

Mr Grey entered public life in the parliament of 1784, as member for his own county of Northumberland . . . . [**197**] His maiden speech was *against* free trade, *against* the commercial treaty with France, *against* the only liberal measure of the eighteenth century in trade. With the impetuosity of a young man he even questioned the patriotism of the manufacturers, anxious at all cost for export and a market. But although, in 1827, he would not, as a matter of tact, have done this, yet there is no sentiment in his first speech which does not justify his almost solitary secession from the Whigs at the time of Mr. Canning's Corn Law relaxations.[56] His mind was full, from first to last, of those traditions which held agriculture to be the sole great gentlemanly interest, and the country party the only party in the state. [**198**] . . .

In the great schism which the French Revolution caused in the Whig Party, Mr. Grey remained true to his own instincts, and to Mr. Fox.[57] Sanguine and chivalric both in manners and in language, he knew that his adoption of popular principles would never confound *him* with the populace. He seemed like a baron of Runnymeade, a Paladin at the head of the people, all the more of a Paladin from the contrast. Even as a **[199]** 'friend of the people,' he was distinguished for his haughtiness; he took pains to show that he used the *manants* about him only as instruments and tools. And yet, if Lord Grey had been born a plebian, his speech would have been rude and licentious, his conduct turbulent and seditious; he might have inveighed at a rotunda, or belonged to a conspiracy. There was something of Cobbett in his temper.[58] **[200]** . . .

. . . During that interval, **[204]** from George the Third's derangement in October 1810, down to Mr. Perceval's assassination in May, 1812, . . . Lord Grey might have been Premier at any moment on conditions. But his attitude was rather that of a master than a servant, of a dictator than a minister. He wanted to school the monarchy into what Mr. Disraeli would call the dogeship. . . . **[205]**

The prevalence of what we . . . call the Banausic principle, was to effect a change in Lord Grey's application of his politics, if not in his politics themselves. When the Ryders became grandees, and the vote of a Pepper Arden was as good as that of a Devonshire; when the aristocracy of the robe already threatened to swamp the Upper House, Lord Grey began to draw distinctions.[59] He did not include the new men, when he spoke of standing by his order. The absurd and exaggerated pretensions, too, of the pseudo-aristocrats did much to increase his disgust. An exclusive dignity, which the Shrewsburys and Somersets, the Newcastles and Bedfords, had never ventured to assert, was arrogated by the ostentatious *parvenus*, whom the insanity of George the Third, and the bigotry of the nation, had hatched into so gaudy a corruption. Their claims as compared with those of the old Whig magnates, were as ridiculous as the pretensions of the servants in 'High Life Below Stairs,' or those of a section of Anglican religionaries, who would fain make Leeds their Rome, and who claim for the Establishment **[207]** prerogatives which Rome, with all Christendom to back her, hardly ever dared to assume.[60] But the country was with them, the heir presumptive was with them; and the nobleman of Brookes's was forced to look elsewhere than to his cousins and his boroughs for aid. He was compelled to ally himself with the middle class, to adopt their opinions, to compromise with their prejudices, to avail himself of their energies, in order to conquer and beat down the Plebian Aristocracy which governed. **[208]** . . .

This is not the occasion, nor have we here the space to do justice to the unswerving onwardness, stout heart, and inflexible courage with which Lord Grey carried the great measure [of parliamentary reform] to a successful issue. Through opposition, and hostility, and intrigue, and waverings, he held on his high course. His popularity among all classes, except the spurious aristocracy whom he conquered, was such as no minister had ever before obtained. The king, the people, the middle class, all but the few and privileged were with him. And even among these, there were many who could not see without some emotion the 'old man eloquent,' who had half a century before voted for Mr. Pitt's Reform Bill, who had never varied, or flinched, or hesitated. . . .[61] **[211]**

. . . [Lord Grey] was the last type of that old party honour which the eclecticism of our day has now withered and destroyed. . . . He was as sensitively alive to the honour of his followers as of his own; the trustee of their character, and the defender of their faith. . . .

Like the Gonfalonier of the Italian Republics,[62] the standard, with all its alliances, and all its feuds, had been committed to his charge, and he determined to sustain it without yielding to a foe, and without a stain upon its folds. The old Whig traditions were preserved by him pure and intact, sacred and complete. Their greatest modern illustrations were of his achievement. The Abolition of the Slave trade in 1807, when he was foreign secretary; the Abolition of Slavery in 1834, when he was Prime Minister; their long and magnanimous exile from power, from 1806 down to 1830, for the sake of emancipation and of Ireland; the Reform Bill, which he proposed in one century and which he carried in another. Such were among the triumphs of his magnificent career. Rare trophies, and almost unexampled in one public life! **[217]** . . .

. . . We have made these remarks in haste, and with a negligence which at some future period we shall care to improve. But, in a periodical which would fain reflect the opinions of the more Catholic and large-hearted among our English Universities, it seemed to us a gentle office, and not unworthy of a young undertaking, to offer to greatness an early tribute of the coming fame. 'The youth of a nation are the trustees of posterity.' . . .

We have written, too, without hope or passion, without fear or prejudice. Or if there be a prejudice, it is [not] one which might have persuaded us to judge harshly and speak unfavourably. We have not belonged to the same army, nor worn the same uniform, nor respected the same standard. But it would be absurd to measure the parts of the general of an opposing army, by the ribaldry and slang of one's own camp followers . . . . We believe, on the contrary, that ever since the beginning of the Parliamentary system, there have been, perhaps as long as it lasts, there may also be, two great parties. None but an Irishman can believe, that the one is absolutely right, or the other absolutely wrong. Each, rather, has had in its custody a true faith. Each represents a necessity for England. The creed of this is love of antiquity and abhorrence of disorder, the creed of that, desire for improvement, and detestation of oppression. To different temperaments each has its particular charms. One of our northern voyagers has declared that he could distinguish the character of his men, by their habits during leisure. Those of a romantic or melancholy disposition were wont to linger at the stern of the vessel, and interchange regrets for old times and their native land; others, of bolder and more sanguine temper, would crowd about the forecastle, and stimulate each other with hopes of new excitement and fresh adventure.[63] Such as this is the dissidence of public men. The pensive and superstitious, **[218]** the chivalrous and the formal, the rich and the contented, the timid and the cautious, are alike natural Conservatives. On the other hand, the ardent and unsettled, the visionary and the optimist, the poor and the persecuted, cast themselves at once into the Movement. Each party has much to stir the heart, and move the imagination. Each boasts its noble army of martyrs . . . . Each has its goodly fellowship of prophets. Each, too, has its heroic succession . . . . Among these . . . Lord Grey . . . will rank conspicuous and high: Partisan, Politician, Country Gentleman, Patrician, minister, Speaker, Statesman, he was always admirable – a great man who has left a great example. **[219]**

George Smythe, 'George Canning'[64]

[. . .] Eloquence brought to perfection, is the most arduous, and, perhaps, the noblest of arts. In its abuse, as in the abuse of any other great instrument of power, there is a very deep depravity; but in its right use and legitimate intention there is high merit, and there are sublime rewards. To persuade others at will, is surely an art of great difficulty and of great power; to persuade them ever towards the right and honourable course, towards their own true and ultimate welfare, – spiritualizes that difficulty, and makes the orator an admirable and majestic character, who performs great feats for an end noble, beneficent, and holy. . . . **[399]**

The Orator . . . can act on men's appreciation of advantage. His intellect has achieved great things, and has mastered one important region of his Art. But a new and a fairer territory, among men, opens before him: he must learn to govern and to influence their susceptibility of enjoyment.

The chief element which acts on that susceptibility is Beauty. On this ambrosial element lives, for the most part, each liberal Art. The more ideal school of painting inhales the breath of inspiration from Beauty. Sculpture studies and reproduces Beauty. Music is Beauty. There is besides a terrible

Beauty, called sublimity, known to each liberal art, and which, under Burke's correction, addresses itself also to our susceptibility of pleasure, not of pain.[65]

We have not yet mentioned Poetry, because, in our opinion, the other Arts, always excepting Eloquence, are not worthy to be named along with that divine and infallible form of Beauty. And here is the reason why we hold that opinion. Of Beauty there are two kinds, the spiritual and the material; to the former belongs the beauty of the mind. Noble sentiments, pathetic recollections, sweet associations, pure and exalted ideas, lofty achievements, great and good characters, memorable actions – lives divinely led even to their consummation – fidelity, loyalty, morality, the Truths of Revelation, the rhapsodies of the Prophets, our aspirations after an immortal destiny – these things possess an *immaterial* beauty. They possess a beauty independent [**402**] of the outer forms by which they may be accompanied, a beauty of subtle and imperishable essence, which is seen by the mind, and which escapes the sense; which is seen and which is loved by the mind.

Now, Poetry can express with equal ease both these kinds of beauty. – That more excellent kind of beauty which we have just described, and a Beauty less excellent and less glorious, – a sensible, material, palpable, and earthly beauty – are (each in its several modifications) alike the province of Poetry. But Sculpture, Music, and Painting, are nearly unable to seize spiritual beauty; these Arts are essentially of this earth, earthly. There is, then, a kind of beauty beyond their reach; but no kind of beauty is beyond the reach, or outside the dominion of Poetry. A fair and noble head; the divine indweller is as suitably revealed, as the perishable dwelling. Poetry, in fine, possesses all the beauty which the other Arts possess. But there is a beauty which the other Arts possess not, and which Poetry possesses; and it is exactly that beauty which is, in every respect, the noblest, the most excellent, and the most divine. In addition to all this, it might be remarked, that Poetry invades in some degree the immediate province of Music; and, like Music, has the charm of sweet sounds.

. . . It is clear, for we now return to the Orator, that the discipline he must have practised for the acquisition of the talents necessary in addressing the utilitarian side of questions, in influencing his listeners by their appreciation of advantage, is precisely that discipline which is the least calculated to develop his power of addressing their sense of Beauty, and of ruling them by their susceptibility of pleasure. He must therefore be on his guard, lest in acquiring one faculty essential to the orator, he unfit himself for the acquisition of another, equally essential. The orator must have a very well-balanced mind, and doubtless this is the reason why no great orator was ever known to go mad. . . . His genius is well-balanced; he must have the precise and practical mind of the mechanician, but enlarged, and fired, and beautified by the touch of divine Poesy; he must understand metaphysics like any schoolman, but manners [403] and externals must be as familiar to him as to any comedian; his intellect must be patient and accurate enough to pore into the minutest details of analysis; but he will not get mad over them, like the watch-maker, for they constitute not his whole being, and other pursuits are at his elbow, to whisper him away to more genial and more lovely avocations. His understanding must be able to soar into the highest regions of pneumatological abstraction; but it will not be for the sake of soaring: the quarry must be struck, and then, obedient to the call, the falcon will return to the wrist; will not sail down the wind, nor lose itself in protracted aberrations. His arguments must be carefully sharpened; they may be winged with wit, they may be gemmed with imagery, but passion must shoot them home. . . . [404]

. . . Thus, then, we have seen, that in order to attain excellence in the art of persuasion, the various qualities which the mechanical, and which the liberal Arts severally demand, are here alike and simultaneously necessary. . . . Then comes a fresh world of difficulties; the intimate acquaintance with the more immediate details of his own Art. [405] He must have a perfect style; an attainment which requires exquisite taste, as well as the most persevering pains . . . . And in addition to all this, he must, of course, thoroughly understand the mechanical construction of a discourse, and all the minor details of that *art within his art*, which is called Rhetoric.

. . . This . . . discipline being passed, and few there are that pass it, knowledge of the subject under discussion is essential. . . . That subject may be any. Universal information, then, not certainly of a detailed or analytic kind, but rather of a large and synthetical philosophy, like that which Lord Bacon possessed, ought to be added to the profound artistic knowledge which the Orator must have previously attained. [406]

. . . The perfect Orator, such as we have described him, is the natural leader of his country, and one of the rulers of his race. He possesses real power; the earth wears his shadow, the destinies of mankind feel his weight. Kings and commanders, though always surrounded with the emblems of authority, are not always in a position to exert it, still less to exert it against the combined strength of circumstances and of passions; least of all, in the heat and fury of some national mania. Yet these emergencies uncrown not the orator;

He rides in the whirlwind, and directs the storm.

They are but as an element to his genius. Kings may be dethroned, ministers dismissed; but what can unthrone or dismiss a potentate who carries his authority in his own mind? Nor is this more than ministerial, this more than royal power his only consolation: it is perhaps still more consoling to human frailty to reflect that all has been gained by his own exertions; that he inherited no advantages, that 'the honourable toil' which, [**407**] with unwearied perseverance, prepared the ground and sowed the seed, was alone, under God, to be thanked for 'the honourable reward.'

. . . But, after all, what is power? a thing of which a noble mind never for a moment thought, – except as the soldier thinks of the musket, as the husbandman thinks of the plough, as the painter thinks of the brush, and the sculptor of the chisel. It is but an instrument to be used for the achievement of a great and noble end, for the promotion of the cause of universal order, for the advantage of one's country, for the improvement of one's fellow-creatures, and, be it even said, for the celebration of the glory of Him who made them. [**408**]

. . . In this portrait of an ideal perfection, there are lineaments which remind you of George Canning. To say that he was a perfect Orator, would be over the truth. But to call him the last of the rhetoricians would be quite impertinent, and would betray a deplorable ignorance of the principles of sound criticism. He was much more than a rhetorician, he was a great Orator . . . .

. . . Canning stirred the heart of England to the very depths; he evoked a spirit which is not yet laid, and which now . . . continues to animate a considerable portion of the empire. In life he continued to grow more powerful, by a steady progression, even to the end; and he died, ruler of England – ruler of England amid circumstances of peculiar and pre-eminent difficulty, by the sole ascendant of his individual energies, and of his single genius; deserted, betrayed, beset on every side, but undismayed, constant, invincible, victorious. Sometimes, as his glorious career waxed towards its meridian, in which it was abruptly closed by no mortal enemy, but by the hand of God – sometimes in his life, we say, the torrent of evil times bore down those august fortunes; but still his star ever prevailed against adversity. . . . Such was the career of George Canning. Through the mere ascendant of his individual character, unaided by connexions, by wealth, or by the charms of an ancestral name,[66] he infused new life into a failing cause, and upheld, even to his death, the standard which had been entrusted [**409**] to his gallant and knightly keeping. He upheld it to his death, not in a wavering or a doubtful eminence, but in victory ever, with stern triumph, against a world. We use the expression, 'against a world,' advisedly; for, though many sympathies now cling to the memory of George Canning, though the very nation wept at his untimely death, it was not exactly so when Canning was amongst us.

After the description which we have given of the requisites for Eloquence, there could hardly be an eulogy more significant than to say that Canning was eminently eloquent. He was indeed a great master of this great Art of persuasion. ... But ... Canning deserves a still greater respect, – a still more splendid encomium. Not only did he persuade men, but he persuaded them towards noble purposes; and though his words often failed of an immediate result, they yet failed not of an immediate impression. They prepared the way for beneficent times. We talk not of party objects, when we say that Canning persuaded men towards noble purposes. We willingly hand over to the secular arm of political hostility his defence of Old Sarum,[67] though, by-the-by, were he here, we know not the secular arm which would venture to chastise him. But we talk rather of that sympathy for the oppressed which glowed so vividly in his own bosom, and which he diffused so largely; – we remember rather his energetic, his solemn advocacy of the poor Africans' cause, as well as the part which he took in preparing the way for the emancipation of the Catholics. We remember rather the share which he had in the most glorious and protracted contest ever waged by England, – a contest, in spite of wounds received and losses incurred, productive of so many happy results to this country, to Europe, and to the universe; a contest which retrieved the cause of order and humanity against the utmost might of anarchical aggression, placed England in the vanguard of progress, of civilization, and of power; and restored freedom to prostrate nations, while it secured lasting tranquillity to mankind. In these transactions, we hardly know which to admire most, the sound and right-hearted principles, the statesmanlike penetration, or the great and divine eloquence of George Canning. Certainly this country may well be proud of having **[410]** possessed him; it never possessed a more active, perhaps not often a more able servant; it never possessed a more disinterested, or patriotic, or enthusiastic minister.

... This man ... was as generous as Lord Byron; as business-like as Sir Robert Peel; as bold as Chatham; as gentle as Wilberforce; as witty and as eloquent as Sheridan ... .[68] Who more refined in manners, who more bearable even in the provoked sallies of his impetuous, but manly temper? Who more mindful of services? – while of injuries who more forgetful? Who more unblemished in honour? more fair and gallant in contest; in friendship more steadfast or more true? **[411]**

Notes to Part III

1. *House of Commons Debates*, 67 c928–30.
2. Ibid., 70 c745–52.
3. Ibid., 70 c919–24. Pitt's intention was that the union of the British and Irish parliaments in 1801 would be accompanied by measures removing penalties against Roman Catholics. Canning was a strong proponent of Catholic Emancipation and maintained this stance in the face of virulent opposition from members of his own party.
4. That is, the Roman Catholic Seminary where the members of the priesthood were trained.
5. Ibid., 72 c1158–69. In response to Milnes' claim T. B. Macaulay declined to follow the course 'traced out to us by my hon. Friend opposite, with all the authority which he, as he justly states, derived from his venerable youth' (ibid., 72 c1169–70).
6. Manners 1841.
7. *House of Commons Debates*, 69 c525–6. The debate arose when William Sharman Crawford, MP for Rochdale, sought leave to introduce a bill to 'secure the full representation of the people'.
8. Young England (1845) 7 (15 February), p. 106.
9. See Manners' speech on Mortmain, above pp. 88–93.
10. Smythe 1847.
11. These references are to a plan to place educational resources raised through the poor rate under the control of the Church of England. This measure was opposed vigorously by Protestant dissenters.
12. Cf. Manners' views on the enslavement of the Church to the State, above, pp. 85–6.
13. John Arthur Roebuck, MP (1801–79) was closely associated with a group of 'philosophic radicals' of Benthamite leanings.
14. A series of acts of parliament that made it necessary for those non-Anglican Protestants who wished to exercise political rights to subscribe nominally (and, it was thought, insincerely) to the theological tenets of the Anglican Church of England.
15. Manners 1841.
16. Smythe 1844.
17. Etienne-François, Duc de Choiseul (1719–85) was Louis XV's chief minister from 1758 to 1770. Michel Le Tellier (1603–85) was Secretary of State for War under Louis XIV, a post later held by both his son and grandson.

18. Under the restored monarchy members of the Upper Chamber were nominated by the king from lay, military and religious elites.
19. The 'Fronde': a noble revolt which took place between 1648 and 1653. François de Bassompierre (1579–1646), Marshall of France; Cardinal Jules Mazarin (1602–61), Minister of Louis XIV; Henri, duc de Montmorenci (1596–1632), Marshall of France; Cardinal Richelieu (1585–1642), Minister to Louis XIII and Louis XIV.
20. That is, between the stock exchange (the Bourse), representing financial interests, and trading interests; the Rue Quincampoix was a major thoroughfare in the commercial heart of the city.
21. In June 1791 Louis XVI and members of his family attempted to flee from an increasingly threatening situation in Paris. The royal party was recognized and stopped at the town of Varennes in north-eastern France and was sent back to the Tuileries, the royal place in Paris. Sanilas, Comte de Clermont-Tonné (1757–92) was a leading figure in the noble opposition to royal policy that emerged in 1789. In 1789 the Vicomte de Noailles (1756–1804) seized the initiative in proposing the renunciation of noble privileges. Noailles was notorious for his lack of landed property; his nickname was 'Jean sans-terre'.
22. The Code Napoléon introduced during the Empire replaced pre-revolutionary legal systems, including those that gave special rights to the nobility; it was maintained by Napoleon's successors.
23. That is, the royal place from the working-class quarters of Paris.
24. Smythe refers to aristocratic opposition to the July monarchy installed following the revolution of 1830.
25. Disraeli 1845, Bk I, ch. 3.
26. That is, with the court-in-exile of James II in France.
27. Young England (1845) 13 (29 March).
28. Manners 1841.
29. Smythe 1844.
30. Sir Peter Lely (1618–80), portrait painter. George Villiers, second Duke of Buckingham (1628–87), was a favourite of Charles II. The first and second Earls of Rochester were important figures at the courts of Charles I and Charles II. The Villerois played a leading role in French politics from the sixteenth century. Nicolas (1598–1685), Duke of Villerois, and his son François (1644–1730) were marshals of France. The Rohans (originally from Brittany) were leading members of the French nobility from the eleventh century; they were prominent at court, in the Church and in the armed forces. William Wycherly (1640?–1716), a dramatist, was a favourite at the court of Charles II; his work is contrasted unfavourably with that of the French dramatist Jean-Baptiste Poquelin (1622–73), 'Molière'. 'Montespan' is the Marquise Françoise Athenaïs de Rochechquart de Mortemat (1640–1707), mistress of Louis XIV. Barbara Villiers, Duchess of Cleveland (1641–1709), was a mistress of Charles II.
31. Anthony Ashley Cooper (1621–83), first Earl of Shaftesbury, was active in the recall of Charles II in 1660. Although he promoted toleration, he also encouraged the Popish Plot of 1678 and sought to exclude the Duke of York (later James II), a Roman Catholic, from the throne. Sir Thomas Wentworth (1593–1641), first Earl of Strafford, was a statesman and soldier. Having originally been opposed to the king's policy Strafford entered his service in 1629 and became his chief advisor; he was lord lieutenant of Ireland from 1639. His execution, to which Charles gave formal agreement by signing the Bill of Attainder, is often described as an act of 'judicial murder'. John Hampden (1594–1643) was prominent in the parliamentary opposition to Charles I after 1627, particularly in the 'Ship Money' case. Although

he played a leading role in the impeachment of Strafford in 1641, Hampden opposed the Bill of Attainder. Jacques Bénigne Bossuet (1627–1704), Archbishop and royal advisor, was a theologian, philosopher and historian of great note. François De Salignac De La Motle Fenelon (1651–1715), archbishop; a friend and disciple of Bossuet, he was also a famous literary figure.

32. Smythe 1844.
33. This incident is recorded in James Boswell's *Life of Johnson* (1791), Part I (Boswell 1979, p. 39).
34. Smythe 1844.
35. Lord Cornbury, grandson of the first Earl of Clarendon was a member of a leading Cavalier family. His father remained a staunch Jacobite. Sir Thomas Osbourne (1631–1712), Earl of Danby, Marquis of Carmarthen and Duke of Leeds from 1694, greatly enriched himself while in the service of Charles II. John Churchill (1648–1730), first Duke of Marlborough, was a soldier and politician. His sister Arabella Churchill was James II's mistress. A number of Townsends, beginning with Charles (1674–1738), the second Viscount, played prominent roles in government after the Glorious Revolution of 1688/9. Charles' father (Sir Horatio Townsend (1630?–87)) worked to ensure the Restoration of Charles II and was rewarded by being elevated to the peerage in 1661.
36. Sir George Saville (1633–95), Marquis of Halifax, was originally ennobled by Charles II in 1668. He attempted to forge a compromise between James II and his opponents in Parliament; when this failed he formally requested William and Mary to accept the Crown in 1689. Robert Spencer (1640–1702), second Earl of Sunderland, had gained influence under Charles II; he was a confidant of James II while making overtures to William of Orange. His craftiness, insincerity and rapacity were notorious.
37. The League, which was led by William of Orange (William III), gave its name to a war fought from 1689 to 1697 between the English and Dutch on one side and Louis XIV and his allies on the other.
38. Henrietta of England (1644–70) was the daughter of Charles I of England and his wife Henrietta of France. Bossuet, who had been her spiritual adviser, gave the oration on 21 August 1670; it is regarded as the finest of his prose writings.
39. Manners 1841.
40. Disraeli 1845, Bk IV, ch. 14. The context of this remark is the 'Bed Chamber Plot' of May 1839: Peel refused to take office unless the Queen agreed to make changes to her household to signify her support for him.
41. As reported in the *Kentish Observer*, 14 January 1841. This speech, made during Smythe's first election campaign, caused a minor sensation, being widely and favourably noticed in a range of London papers: the *Argus*; *Morning Herald*; *Morning Post*; *Standard* and *The Times*. Extracts from these papers were published in the other local Tory paper, the *Kentish Gazette* on 19 January 1841.
42. The text is taken from the report in the *Manchester Guardian*, 5 October 1844.
43. For Manners' interest in historical research and writing see Whibley 1925.
44. Alexander Dyce (1798–1869) was a celebrated Shakespearean scholar and critic. 'Professor Willis' is probably Robert Willis (1800–75), Jacksonian professor of applied mechanics at Cambridge and author of a number of technical works on medieval architecture.
45. A reference to Pugin's *Contrasts*; see above, pp. 23, 96.
46. *Manchester Guardian*, 5 October 1844. This speech was reproduced in Young England (1885) and in *The Importance of Literature*.
47. Smythe 1844.

48. Young England (1845) 4 (25 February).
49. Disraeli 1844, Bk II, ch. 5.
50. Issued by Sir Robert Peel in 1834 to point the way for the transformation of the old Tory party into what became known as the Conservative Party.
51. Manners 1846. Manners' articles appeared after the onset of the crises caused by Peel's announcement in 1845 of his decision that the Corn Laws should be repealed; it sets this declaration, and responses to it, in a context that went back to 1841 and concerned not just the termination of protection accorded to wheat growers, but a general movement to eliminate a wide range of protective tariffs. Peel's budget of 1842 modified the sliding scale of duties applied to imported corn in a liberal direction; it also removed prohibitory duties and drastically reduced the duties on a large number of imports, particularly raw materials and primary foodstuffs. Further liberalization occurred as part of Peel's second free-trade budget of 1845. The Corn Laws themselves were finally repealed in June 1846, following the announcement of new free-trade proposals in January of that year.
52. Following widespread agitation in the north of England Lord Ashley introduced an amendment to legislation before Parliament in 1844 to reduce working hours for young people to ten hours a day. Since this group was an essential part of the workforce it was recognized that the measure would restrict factory hours in general. Legislation including the amendment was finally passed in 1847.
53. Robert Christopher and William Miles represented rural areas and were closely identified with the landed interest. Sir James Graham MP (1792–1861), Home Secretary under Peel 1841–6, was a leading spokesman for the Conservative Party in the House of Commons. During the period before Peel announced his conversion to a complete system of free trade, the Conservative position on this issue was under constant challenge from Richard Cobden MP (1804–65), a leading figure in the Anti-Corn Law League, and Charles Pelham Villiers MP (1802–98), who moved annual resolutions against the Corn Laws in the House of Commons from 1838 until their repeal in 1846.
54. These references are to parts of Peel's speech of which this article is an ostensible review (Peel 1846). In 1796 William Pitt the Younger (1759–1806), then Prime Minister, had proposed a significant reform of the Poor Laws. Pitt stressed that the poor had a right to relief and opposed the removal of paupers to their parish of settlement. He wished to provide a parochially administered system of superannuation and proposed that the operation of the poor relief system should be overseen by 'visitors' drawn from among the gentry; see Erhman 1983, pp. 472–4. Many features of this scheme, which was never put to the vote, would have been attractive to Manners.
55. Smythe 1845a.
56. In 1827, George Canning, who was Smythe's idol (see below, pp. 152–6) liberalized the protective duties on imported wheat by introducing a sliding-scale which linked the degree of protection to the prices fetched by home-grown wheat.
57. That is Charles James Fox (1749–1806), the leader of the Whig Party in the late eighteenth and early nineteenth centuries. The party was weakened greatly by defections to the Tories of those who regarded Fox's radical and pro-French views as untenable in the wake of the French Revolution.
58. That is, William Cobbett (1762–1835), a radical politician and journalist who was an inveterate critic of aristocratic and commercial corruption in politics.
59. Richard Pepper Arden (1745–1804), a successful lawyer, attorney- and solicitor-general and Lord Chief Justice of the Common Pleas, became Baron Alvanley in 1801; Sir Dudley Ryder (1691–1756), also attorney- and solicitor-general, and then

Lord Chief Justice of the King's Bench, was the first Baron Ryder of Harrowby. His son became Earl of Harrowby and Viscount Sandon in 1809. Smythe uses the French distinction between 'aristocracies of the robe' (those ennobled for administrative and legal service) and 'aristocracies of the sword' to contrast these families with the long-established houses mentioned in this paragraph who were ennobled for military service. Smythe, whose family was in embarrassingly dire financial straits in the eighteenth century (his grandfather had to avail himself of a fund to assist impoverished members of the Irish nobility), shared Grey's prejudices against newcomers in the nobility. In a letter to Disraeli, Smythe poured scorn on the pretensions of those being talked of as candidates for inclusion in the Order of the Garter. One of his targets on this occasion were the Bentincks (the family name of the Dukes of Bedford) who befriended Disraeli and assisted him in the purchase of Hughenden Manor (Hugenden Mss, 144/1/fo. 226, 20.10.1844).

60. A reference to the strength of Anglo-Catholicism in that city.
61. William Pitt the Younger made unsuccessful attempts to carry a modest measure of parliamentary reform in 1783 and 1785; he was frustrated by opposition within his own party; see Erhman 1969, pp. 226–8.
62. That is, the leading officer, usually appointed from among the aristocratic element in these states.
63. Perhaps a reference to Sir John Franklin (1789–1847), who left on his last and fateful voyage to northern Canada in May 1845. The editor has not found this observation in Franklin's accounts of his earlier voyages; it may have been made in a periodical or in speech.
64. Smythe 1845c.
65. Edmund Burke, *A Philosophical Enquiry into the Origin of Our Ideas of the Sublime and Beautiful* (1756).
66. Canning's father died when he was a year old; his mother supported herself by working as an actress.
67. Old Sarum, a notorious 'rotten borough' with no residents, lost its parliamentary representation as a result of the Reform Act of 1832. Canning defended 'rotten boroughs' on the grounds that they provided a way in which men of talent could come into Parliament under the patronage of their owners thus avoiding the uncertainty and expense of a contested election.
68. William Pitt, the Elder, first Earl of Chatham (1708–87), a leading figure in mid-century politics, was Prime Minister and served in a number of administrations; William Wilberforce (1759–1833) was the leading parliamentary promoter of the anti-slavery movement; Richard Brinsley Sheridan (1751–1816) was a noted playwright and politician.

PART IV

Contemporaries on
Young England

The ideas of Young England figures provoked a wide range of responses from contemporaries. Some critics were dismissive, patronizing or hostile, but there was also a great deal of sympathy for Young England's aspirations. Contemporaries noted the enthusiasm and freshness that Young England brought to the parliamentary and extra-parliamentary debates and commented on its distinctive sense of political style. Some critics were offended at the pretensions of Young England figures and questioned its claim to represent a new departure in political thought and action. The movement's fascination with traditional conceptions of authority, and its engagement with the 'Condition of England question' was discussed widely, and so too were the literary interests and attainments of its leading members. It was widely recognized that Young England writers regarded their literary works as an integral part of the political and social causes that they promoted.

I   The Spirit of Young England

(i) Young England's Style

[Anon.], 'Benjamin D'Israeli and the New Generation'[1]

. . . Between Mr. D'Israeli's political and literary course of action, affinities and analogies are often discoverable. As the wondrous Tale of Alroy might be said to be a combination of poetry and prose, so the wondrous creed, to the exposition of which all ears, long and short, are opened in the present day, may be described as a combination of the [**499**] elder Toryism, as it flourished prior to the era of social corruption, and the latest Radicalism, as it overlooks the factory and the union work-house, and dances round the May-pole to the pipe and tabor.

Young England, the representative of our New Generation, wears a velvet vest and leather leggings; on the hand which he sets to the plough, a diamond ring is glistening; he has a coronet on his head, and treads the mire in clouten shoon: he breakfasts on a *paté de foie gras*, and three pints of oatmeal porridge. But there is body as well as soul in him nevertheless; a good deal of consistency, in spite of the anomalies; determined energy of tongue and action, and plenty of life – while he lives. [**500**]

[Anon.], 'Mr Disraeli's *Sybil*'[2]

The previous notice of *Coningsby*, and of its eloquent author, enables [**541**] us, on the present occasion, to swerve from mere analysis and tedious description, and to dwell more upon those original and sparkling topics eliminated by Young England, out of an age of political materialism, of confused purposes, and perplexed intelligence. The chief of these topics is the condition of the poor . . . . [I]n the scope given to the subject, the magnitude of the principles involved, the evils and the sufferings denounced, and the themes proposed for their mitigation . . . Young England carries with it an overwhelming superiority. [**542**]

. . . Mr. Disraeli believes that we live in an age when, to be young and to be indifferent, can no longer be synonymous; and it is his persuasion that great results can only be brought about by the energy and devotion of youth, prompted by that noble spirit and gentle nature which is embodied in a Sybil . . . . [**544**]

(ii)   Nobility, Heredity and Religion

[Anon.], Review of *Historic Fancies*[3]

[. . .] Aristocracy is one of the superstitions of Young England. Singular contradictions of opinion seem to exist amongst the disciples upon this subject; but 'gentle blood' and 'hereditary succession,' and all that fine and delicate energy which springs from high breeding and habitual command, always excite their admiration. . . . [**528**]

It requires very little political sagacity to discern through this congenial historical fantasy, the roots of that devoted loyalty which flourishes so luxuriantly in the affections of Young England. That chivalry of character which burns in her verse, which is so fond of taking up hopeless questions, which sympathises so eagerly with the friendless and the poor, and which, in spite of all the ludicrous and incongruous associations of ideas it is apt to conjure up, is animated by a sincere zeal and the warmest generosity – that peculiar and solitary chivalry of our time never appears to greater advantage than when it is enlisted on behalf of the throne. This is a legitimate topic, surrounded by the most inspiring lore, fenced in by gorgeous and valiant memories, and sanctified by time and the silent accumulation of human assent. It has been objected to the New Generation that they are fond of defending James II, and of expressing their sympathy generally for the Stuarts. They who make the objection, see nothing in the ardour with which the Martyr and the Exile are upheld in these fantastic writings, but a sinister proof of the Puseyite spirit;[4] overlooking the pervading sentiment of legitimacy, which is paramount to all others, and for the maintenance of which, Mr. Smythe is not unwilling to risk the whole social fabric and official organisation of France. There may be a strong leaven of the Puseyite spirit in that sympathy – but it is not for Tractarian ends it is so eloquently poured out in startling measures and allegories, oriental in their pomp of diction. It would be a great injustice to this young, and, as yet, rather visionary school of statesmen, not to acknowledge a higher and more enduring principle in their labours than that of endorsing the crotchets of the University. Tractarians they may be, and are – but with different degrees of faith, and probably, different versions of the disputed articles. But it is not for this they solicit charity for Charles and James – but because those luckless princes are the great examples in our history of sacrilegious violence offered to the person of the sovereign. They would have the sovereign sacred from the rude touch of the populace – tabooed even in the midst of wrongs and crimes. . . . [**530**]

. . . Mr. Smythe will scarcely think we throw any slight upon his principles if we conclude by saying that we have a deeper faith in his poetry than his politics. We often discern the influence of the former giving a palpable but unconscious direction to the latter. His poetry often speaks when he believes it to be the voice of his politics, – and it will be heard when the doctrines of Young England shall have lapsed into oblivion. We are too confident of the reality of his genius not to be quite sure that it will long survive the vicissitudes of party. [**534**]

2 Literature and Politics

(i) *'Literary Legislators'*

[Anon.], 'Mr. B. Disraeli'[5]

I

. . . The general principle of a party, few in number but rich in talent, and who have been hitherto undervalued, will be found in this remarkable and extravagant production [*The Revolutionary Epic*[6]]; and Mr. Disraeli's ideas of Young Englandism, as afterwards explained in *Coningsby* and *Sybil*, are here struggling into light amidst many weed-like absurdities. This is one of the evidences . . . of the consistency and sincerity of Mr. Disraeli as a political thinker. [**84**]

. . . In an address to the electors of High Wycombe, which was afterwards published with the title of *The Crises Examined* he more distinctly shadows forth that scheme of Anti-Whig Liberalism, of Tory-Radicalism, of Absolutism and well-governing combined, which forms the only intelligible portion of the theories of the Young England party. [**87**]

II

. . . [Mr Disraeli] was the first to expose that ascendancy of political materialism which has been so fatal to the character of our public men, by lowering the tone of statesmen, and debasing their policy. He has long sustained that an eloquent and indignant protest against that reign of redtapeism – that fruitless incubation of complacent mediocrity, which has, for many years, repressed political genius. He would not worship false gods, but strove to win men back to the true faith. He certainly imparted vigour and coherency to the significant, but uncombined speculations and desires of that band of original thinkers who were so much ridiculed as the Young England party . . . . [207]

[Anon.], 'Lord John Manners'[7]

. . . The political and social aims of Lord John Manners are so totally different from those of any other public man, with one or two exceptions, now in parliament; superficially regarded, they are so hostile to traditionary constitutional notions, as well as to contemporary economical doctrines, as still more to embarrass the subject and increase the difficulty. . . . [321]

[. . .] There are some features in our political system, which, when contrasted with our national greatness, have excited the astonishment of mankind – there are some in our social system which are viewed with sorrow and indignation. The attention of Lord John Manners would seem, from a very early age, to have been arrested by both; and if we may judge from the later fruits of his mind, he has long been struggling, with a deep and earnest purpose, to reconcile inconsistencies, which might, perhaps, have been overlooked but for the frightful evils they have produced; or, not finding a ground of reconciliation, to discover some means by which they might be avoided in a general reconstruction of society, or, in his view, a restoration on its old basis.

We might suppose that Lord John Manners, looking at the working of our constitutional form of government, sees that the popular influence has been carried too far, not, perhaps, for the theory of freedom, but for the practical organisation of society – that events are tending towards a general anarchy of interests and opinions – that each class, each sect, having, through the representative system, a portion of legislative authority in its own hands, is able, if not to secure its own exclusive objects, effectually to obstruct those of others – that in their mutual rivalries a harmonious agreement upon any vital question is as little to be expected as a cheerful or an enforced su⌣mission to authority . . . . [T]he confusion of the only agents of legislation or administration is . . . an absolute paralysis of the governing power, – until, finally, our Ministers, miscalled Rulers, are forced to use a counterfeit authority, which they know is not their own, and of which they are afraid, even while they use it . . . to carry great constitutional questions, or even to effect some of the most obvious suggestions of sound policy . . . . [**322**]

Perhaps we are assuming too much in assigning these views to Lord John Manners; but they are founded on notorious facts, and are consistent with much that he has spoken and written. In fact, we are inclined to believe, that in common with some of the most observant men of his age he is forced to perceive, that from one extreme we are running into another – that in our dread of tyranny we have deprived ourselves of the advantage of legitimate authority. Perhaps, if we could penetrate to the conclusions to which this course of observation may have led . . . Manners, we should find, that to escape from the consequences of the legislative and political anarchy he would take refuge in absolutism. . . . But this, we are persuaded would stop short with theory. As a British nobleman born and bred, and holding all his social privileges, as well as his political rights, under a constitutional form of government, still more as a member of the representative branch of the legislature, he would never, we are convinced, seek so violent a remedy for the evils which he deplores, so long as he could see other means of neutralising their effects. In truth, he does propose a very different kind of remedy, – one which is not only more consistent with the constitution, but which is also quite consonant with the genius of the British people. This brings us to a consideration of another class of questions which have occupied the attention of Lord John Manners, and with regard to which it appears to us that he has given promise of much usefulness to his country.

The social condition of England, but more especially the state of the poorer classes, is a subject which the chief public men of the day dread to probe to its core, while they strive in vain to banish it from legislative consideration. They have startled the public conscience out of its apathy on more than one occasion of warning peril. But class selfishness, and the cumbrousness of our machinery of legislation, have as often lulled that conscience to sleep, or stifled its faint efforts at atonement. . . . We do not like, after having believed for years in principles to which we have [**323**] squared our conduct, to confess that those principles are wrong, or that, in our ignorance, we have misapplied them; and to have to come back to those other principles which we have derided and rejected, only, as it would seem, because they were imposed on us by authority. . . . But a reaction has commenced, a steady and increasing reaction; a reaction of the moral feelings against the cold maxims of selfishness; a reaction whose slow but resistless tide is swelled and upheld by a deep under-current of Christian love and Christian sense of duty. . . .

[. . .] Not the least distinguished amongst the earnest labourers in the cause of social reform is Lord John Manners. . . . [**324**] He is not content with merely cauterising local sores, or with soothing, by temporary expedients, the general irritation produced by the social disease; he would go to the very source, purify the springs, and, however long the process might take, infuse an entirely new life in the organisation. He holds, that our chief social evils arise from the diseased state of the moral nature exhibited by those who, from their having the wealth and station, have therefore the power of producing either good or evil. A neglect of the most plain religious obligations imposed by Christianity, and the substitution for them of certain maxims which, however good for promoting the merely worldly prosperity of individuals or nations, do, nevertheless, exalt selfishness into the law of human conduct; this he conceives to be the great cause which, extending its ramifications from the highest down to almost the lowest classes of society, produces those effects, impalpable at first, but which have increased with frightful rapidity, as the area of competition has been contracted by the increase in population, and the cumulative power of evil stimulated and developed. . . . Nor has the working of this evil . . . stopped with its material consequences. A degraded condition of the labouring classes; insufficient food, bad housing; spiritual as well as physical destitution; these are not the only mischief's that have resulted from the neglect of the Divine behest. Worse than these is the utter severance between the rich and the poor – between employers and the employed – the check to those mutual sympathies arising from protection on the one hand, and affection on the other, which ought to exist between those who are brought into daily contact in such mutual relations. Lord John Manners regards England as a Christian nation unchristianised.

The remedy proposed for these evils by Lord John Manners is a perfectly intelligible one. That it is also the natural remedy may be the reason why, in the unnatural state to which society has reached in this country, it should at present be scouted, and some of its supporters laughed at as visionaries. Among them, let us add, will be found some of the brightest ornaments of this age – some of the holiest and most learned men now living. And here let us pause to correct an error that very commonly prevails with regard to Lord John Manners, and some of those who think with him. They are looked upon as young, inexperienced, enthusiastic visionaries, and, above all, as innovators. Now, this is an error. These young men were not guilty of that rashness and that love of the new which was attributed to them. On the contrary, they were, if anything, somewhat too enamoured of the old. Their process of reasoning was very natural, [**325**] and worthy of much older men. Finding a given state of things existing, which they saw to be bad, they investigated the causes, and believed that they found in the more simple habits of their forefathers a model which, if copied, with many modifications, would effectually reform existing social abuses. They might be right, or they might be wrong; but at least it was a guarantee of their humility that they so loudly proclaimed reliance on the wisdom of their ancestors.

Lord John Manners proposes two classes of remedies. The first is a reorganisation and reinvigoration of the Church of England, to enable it to fulfil those duties as the spiritual instructor of the people for which its large revenues were, or, at least, ought to have been given. . . . [T]he end which Lord John Manners proposes to himself is altogether to raise the moral tone of society, especially in the manufacturing districts, by creating a more general reverence for the Divine will, and a wider and more deeper sense of religious obligations. . . . In an earlier part of this paper it was hinted that Lord John Manners' political theories might lead him up to absolutism, but that he preferred to attain obedience by different means. These, we have alluded to, are the means which he proposes; and, resorted to with due caution, they are, undoubtedly, legitimate means. But he regards this counteraction through the Church as but one portion of his general plan for reuniting in the bonds of harmony, and love, and mutual obligation, the dissevered and mutually repugnant classes of this country. He thinks that political power, through the representative system, has become too much centred in the middle classes; that, under a misconception of the laws of political economy, those classes have constituted themselves the natural enemies of the dependent classes; that they have, perhaps unwillingly, and only under the influence of an insane spirit of competition, established a tyranny of the purse, by which capital, converted, morally speaking, into an abstraction free from all human ties, is made to grind labour, which can never be dissociated from human sympathies, and worse, from human wants. A similar process, he seems to think, has been going on even in the agricultural districts . . . . Thus, whether in one part of the country or in the other, the labouring class came to be socially isolated, to have no friends, to be depressed, and, therefore, to be discontented; to be, in fine, the prey of interested demagogues, or the natural followers of honest and earnest Reformers. Now the idea of Lord John Manners seems to be, that the aristocracy have it in their power to restore the old harmony, if it ever existed, between themselves and the masses. We will not stop to inquire how far lordly jealousy of the growing social importance of men sprung from trade may have helped to [326] bring about this magnanimous purpose. . . . One thing is clear, – if political or social changes, instead of being grudgingly yielded to popular clamour, could take the shape of voluntary and generous concessions, dictated by a spirit of justice, and originated by a desire for the national welfare, much that now darkens the horizon of this country would disappear, and a brighter future might be opened than at present we have any right to hope for. . . .

. . . [W]hatever may be thought by practical men of the value of such proposals as these, to Lord John Manners, at least, is due the praise of advocating them with an earnestness, a sincerity, and a moral energy which have no parallel among living politicians. Let us not forget, that thinkers of the class to which he belongs are essentially engaged in an active protest against the exclusive and tyrannical ascendancy of reason in human affairs. They desire to restore the balance of the human mind; to give to the feelings and sympathies of men their legitimate share of influence; they believe that duty and affection cannot be violently divorced without injury to both. 'Young Englandism' was a sentiment, not a political system. It aimed at moral regeneration, not at working out intellectual problems. It aspired to be, so to speak, a political religion; and its apostles were seized with all that passionate fervour wherewith the preacher enchains the souls of men. . . . [**327**]

[. . .] Without being inconveniently obstinate or self-willed, so as to obstruct legitimate party movements and combinations, . . . [Manners] never hesitates to give utterance to his convictions, however they may clash with the interests or hereditary prejudices of his order. Careless with what time-honoured fallacies or consolidated errors he may interfere, he aims at grand and comprehensive remedies. Round all the lesser circles of circumscribed opinion that have been thrown off at tangents from time to time, in the whirl of affairs, he would describe a larger circle still. He thinks there is efficacy for this object in the old principles and maxims, not forgotten, he hopes, but only laid aside. These he would revive in all their strength, and restore to all their grandeur. He would rebuild the structure of society on the original great design, using as much of existing materials, whether partially organised or disorganised, as can be adopted without interfering with the general plan. Meanwhile he aims at reconciliation, at correcting that mutual repugnance and divergence of opinion and interest in classes, which is the greatest obstacle to unity, whether in spiritual or temporal affairs. We find him supporting earnestly the principle of a property-tax, because he believes it to be a bold, and, as he hopes, a successful attempt to diminish the influence of wealth; to which, and not to that of an aristocracy, he conceives a great portion of our present evils are to be ascribed. Again in . . . [a] speech . . . in which he so deliberately insults His self-crowned Majesty,[8] the People, he declares that he would extend the feeling of responsibility between the rich and the poor, and shorten the interval, now too wide, between those who make the wealth and those for whom it is made. . . . We always find him the advocate of liberality, as distinguished from liberalism; he would voluntarily concede from a sense of justice what others yield reluctantly to clamour. . . . [**336**]

From the foregoing explanation of Lord John Manners' general public conduct, it will seem that we have taken a more liberal view of his position and purposes than will be warranted by the facts of his career. . . . But still, you see the plan, and such a plan contrasts proudly in the imagination with the structures of the minds we now see in active political exercise, that would seem to be the mere chance-work of necessity and circumstances, thrown together to meet emergencies, and only lasting till, in the course of time, they must give way to something greater and more symmetrical. Whether or no Lord John Manners' theory of restoration, under the revived influence of Christianity acting though the Church; of greater obedience by the governed, of greater power with more responsibility in governors; this attempt to extend the patriarchal principle, where it needs must be so difficult to apply it; whether or no these views are capable of adoption, at least they offer a remedy for the increasing anarchy of opinions and interests. . . . It is enough, however, to our purpose, to assert, that in the appearance at the present crisis of a man of the high rank, talents, moral energy, and self-devotion of Lord John Manners, is a political and social phenomena not to be overlooked. Equally remarkable, and, as we conceive, more important, is the advent of such men in connexion with our existing social system. It is not to be lightly passed over, that, at the very period when [**337**] the divergence and mutual repugnance of classes was becoming prospectively dangerous to the common weal, reconcilers and mediators should have sprung up in the ranks of the highest aristocracy, and should have found earnest followers in the Church, in the learned professions, in the press, in the ranks of trade and commerce, ay, and among the common people. . . . [**338**]

[. . .] Once more let us impress on the reader . . . that we have measured Lord John Manners by a higher standard than that afforded by the political materialism of the day. We do not even know that we should desire to see his ideas and proposals transmuted into laws. His political mission is to inspire others with his moral energy and enthusiasm for public virtue. He is the living echo of a voice long unheard, but whose warnings have now become dreadful facts. He points to the future, but with eyes averted to the past. That past may have been a coarse and vicious reality, of which he perceives only a delusive representation; but when we know that the sanctions of existing power are derived from it, we owe something to the man who recalls us to a sense of that which was good in the system of our forefathers; of which we may say that, if much of it has been grossly perverted, so has more been inconsiderately discarded. [**339**]

'Mr. Smythe'[9]

[. . .] Mr. Smythe belongs to a class of minds which, it is to be hoped, represent Young England more faithfully than did the club or clique of young politicians to whom the caprice of party gave that name. It is, let us hope, not the deceptive characteristic of the growing mind of the country, that it is anxious to fling off prejudice – prejudice in favour of the new as much as that on behalf of the old; and to view human affairs by the light of reason, aided by general liberality of sentiment. Their political views represent something better than expediency, something less than faith. They look upon the past as a [**536**] vast collection of facts – sometimes forming invariable precedents – sometimes embodying awful warnings, alike to the bigot as to the speculative philosopher. They enter upon life as on an unexplored region, which the vast changes in the social aspect of society render fit for great experiments; but they would make those experiments, not with the rash arrogance of the empiric, but with the cautious assured audacity of the scientific inquirer. They think that their contemporaries of the elder generation have much to unlearn – that many of their fixed ideas have outlived the circumstances which harmonised with them, and have become worse than useless – that, in fact, prejudice unchallenged constitutes itself the apologist of injustice. The defensive armour wisely adopted at a time of danger may, they conceive, be safely discarded in a period of security, especially as great precautions, where there is no palpable cause for fear, are rightly regarded as evidences of cowardice. They would wish to see the government and all the institutions of the country in the utmost harmony with the altered condition of society, believing such harmony is the best possible guarantee for stability. The difference between them and the expediency-men is that while the latter never see beyond the wants of the hour, and never act till they are forced on from behind, they would take a more prophetic view of the future, and by anticipating its dangers render the present more secure. Of all the young men in parliament who have given utterance to such sentiments, who would have established a species of enlightened Conservatism, as among their opponents there is a striving after a philosophical Radicalism, Mr Smythe seems to be the most practical. In politics he must not be confounded with Lord J. Manners and Mr. Disraeli. For a short time he acted with them, when, with some few others, they constituted the 'Young England' party; but, with the same yearning to nationalise the refinements derivable from aristocratic example, his Liberalism on the other hand was translated into the current language of the people. . . . [537]

(ii)   The Poetry of the New Generation

[Anon.], 'The Prospects of Poetry'[10]

[. . .] If there ever was a time in the whole history of our nation that poetry could cry forth with thrilling inspiration, it is now. Like a young man in disease, England, full of wealth, full of splendour, full of energy, is eaten away by secret corruptions. There is not on the face of the earth a race by nature more honest, more virtuous, more modest; nowhere does the mind of man unite so much strength with so much simplicity, and the heart of woman so much softness with so great a purity: yet there is not a land on earth where there is such manifold corruptions, and such impurities; nowhere is the wretchedness of pauperism so much increased by the absence of all sense of religion; nowhere is morality in its strict sense so little known; nowhere, take them all in all, are the lower orders so wretched, and the higher orders so callous to that wretchedness. In the worst countries of the continent, the poor at least are generally virtuous; you may turn from the corruptions of Paris or Vienna to the simplicity of Brittany or of Tyrol; but from the terrible impurities of London where will you turn?

Were we to enter here into the original cause of the generally acknowledged dearth of all enthusiasm, it would require more space than we can spare; but it is evident that the whole system is wrong, that it had very few elements of health at its birth, and that, by this [time], the few it had have completely disappeared. Political [49] recipes are now exploded: they cannot give content to the poor, they cannot give charity to the rich.

Whilst, however, we are disheartened at the present, we are far from despondent for the future. The present movement – that movement which every body feels around him, which has spread already to every profession and to every rank of life – is but of recent date, and yet it would be difficult to show in our whole history a progress more rapid; and the reason is plain. It is not a struggle for place, it is no mere party squabble. It is a deep conviction that a change is necessary, that this change is to be brought about, not by political caballing, not by hoaxing constituencies, and puzzling majorities; but by appealing carefully and gradually and untiringly to the good sense and to the finer feelings which lurk under the general apathy of the people. The people are degenerate because they have been neglected; cherish and encourage them, and they will become the teachers of their rulers.

. . . The first book in our catalogue, *England's Trust, and other Poems,* though short, is full of a sincere spirit, and of much beauty and appropriateness of expression. It is characteristic of the noble author's piety and kindliness; but his piety is not that of a mere recluse – a strong feeling of patriotism pervades the whole; nor is he insensible to the softer emotions and the poetry of the affections. Still, as we might expect, there is an unworldliness in his poetry, very different from the flesh-and-blood pugnacity of Mr. Smythe, and the more meditative seriousness of Mr. Milnes. . . . **[50]**

There are some people who, if you chance to mention the feudal system, become immediately alarmed.[11] They at once imagine that your object is to restore England to its primitive 'status quo,' to level the manufactures, and to thin the population. For our parts, we think any reasonable man will acknowledge that the feudal system had many advantages, and that if, by considering it, we can establish the excellence of the social sympathy between classes that prevailed under it, we shall have gone a long way towards impressing the public mind with a wish that, without establishing the feudal system, and destroying manufactories, a similar sympathy between the classes of this country would be much preferable to the present state of distrust and contention. **[52]** . . .

Lord John Manners has inscribed his poems to the Honourable Sydney Smythe, who returns the compliment . . . .[12] This interchange of friendly pledges has brought forth from no insignificant an authority the charge of 'cliquism.'[13] We cannot, we acknowledge, see how the fact that two gentlemen holding similar views dedicating their works to each other, can merit for all those who hold the like views the appellation of a 'clique.'[14] If, . . . the accusation . . . is meant to assert that either Lord John Manners, or any of the new generation, are anxious to preserve to their 'clique' a character of exclusiveness, it is an assertion in contradiction to the very sentiments which constitute the strength of the movement, – sentiments of catholic union, and of sympathy between classes. But what, no doubt, was the real motive of so unfounded an accusation, was, that to some men any public display of natural feeling is utterly odious; they can make no allowances for the partiality of a friendship which they cannot comprehend; and, if they have any sincere feelings whatever, they have too 'aristocratic' ideas to let them appear to the vulgar without: they are, in fact, men who believe so little in feeling, that they think it theatrical . . . .

For our part, it is with any thing but an inclination to sneer that we behold the singular unity of purpose and feeling, the evidently heartfelt friendship and affection that exists between the principal men of the 'New Generation.' We consider it a good sign of the times that there should be men, even so small a number, who are linked together by love and sympathy, so impressed with the high duty they have undertaken, that, whilst other parties are barely kept together by the ties of interest or necessity, they remain steadfastly and trustingly united as if they were brothers. [53] . . .

[. . .] We are the more ready to approve such sentiments . . . because we believe that the prevalence of real friendships, something beyond our modern cold and cadenced urbanity, is the sure sign of a sound state of society; if the New Generation introduce a respect for such feelings, it will not be, in our minds, their least service to their country. . . . [55]

To . . . all these writers, great poetic talents must be conceded. They have the first requisite for poets – sincerity. No man, however opposed to their views, or incredulous as to the practicability of their objects, can doubt for a moment that they are serious in their convictions, and earnest in their resolves. They continued perseveringly in the face of the opposition that encountered their first efforts, and it is not likely that now that success is beginning to smile upon their hopes, they will grow less earnest in their faith. Their poetry is, moreover, constant to their objects, for though, the poetic feeling once awakened, their muse often wanders to the groves of love and to the haunts of romance, still she returns again and again to the halls and the monuments and the valleys of England: she is entirely English. . . . To ameliorate the condition of the poor, to renew between the higher and lower orders that natural sympathy without which no society can be sound, to bring back a purer and warmer spirit of religion, – these are objects to the attainment of which a whole life were no unworthy sacrifice. [66]

Those who cannot comprehend that the loyalty of the Jacobites may be praised without a covert attack being implied against Queen Victoria, or that the advantages that existed under the feudal system may be demonstrated without hostility against the present manufactories and commerce – to men of this stamp we have little to say. Nations, like men, have their youth and their maturity. However much we may regret the freshness, the simplicity, and the joyousness of our boyhood, there are very few who, were an angel to descend on earth and offer them the power, would be willing to be boys again. There is an impulse which makes us wish to go forward, and even had we not this impulse, no wise man would look back with regret upon what it is impossible to return to. But though we cannot renew our youth, there is no reason why we should not endeavour to preserve – 'midst the business and the stern occupations of our manhood' – something of our young feelings. The boy grows up and has high and serious duties to perform, but why should he lose the better feelings of his nature as he acquires the influence effectually to exert them? And as for nations, it has yet to be shown that wealth, and commerce, and manufactures, and a high degree of polite refinement, are inconsistent with honesty, morality, generosity, and human love. [**67**]

3 Critical Perspectives

(i) *Spurious Novelty and Partisanship*

John Wilson Croker, 'Young England'[15]

Their number is so small, their views are so vague, and their influence so
slight, that it may seem superfluous to allude to them, but our respect for the
personal character of those amongst them of whom we have any knowledge –
our favourable opinion of their talents though rather, it must be confessed, of
a *belles letters*, than a statesmanlike character – and a strong sympathy with
many of their feelings – induce us to express our surprise and regret that they
should not see, even with their own peculiar views, the extreme inconsistency
and impolicy of endeavouring to create distrust of the only statesman in whom
the great [7] Conservative body has any confidence, or can have any hope.
We make all due allowance for 'young ambition' . . . but we can still find no
sufficient justification for the conduct which these gentlemen have recently
adopted – particularly for their support of Mr. Smith O'Brien's motion[16] – the
most offensive to *Old England* which has been made for many years. We beg
leave, in all kindness, to warn them against being deceived as to the quality
of the notice which their superiority has obtained; it has in it more of wonder
than of respect, and will certainly confer on them no permanent consideration
with any party or any constituency; a few stray and unexpected shots, fired
in the rear of an army, attract more notice than a cannonade in front; but it is
an evanescent surprise, soon forgotten, and remembered only to the
disadvantage of those whose indiscretion created it. . . . [8]

[Anon.], 'A Few Words Anent the Labouring Classes'[17]

[. . .] Since the session came to an end, the leaders of Young England have judged it expedient to take a leaf out of the book which is common to all modern agitators. They went abroad upon a pilgrimage through the provinces; and, now in great towns, now in one or other of the rural districts, they preached up their own views of men and things to audiences as numerous and excitable as they could collect.

To the operatives of Manchester they spoke of clubs of mental culture, of parks, promenades, music, coffee, clean shirts, public baths, and such like. The occupiers and cultivators of the soil they appealed to through the medium of may-poles, cricket-matches, and foot-ball. And all that they said and did had for its object the bringing into closer communion the different orders of society. Their political philosophy, indeed, seems to amount to this: 'Strive, as far as you can, in the management of your social intercourse, to connect the real with the ideal. Break down the barriers which modern times have thrown up between man and man. Cease to regard the class into which you happen to be thrown; think rather of your common country, and in due time it will come to pass that your true interests are the same.' . . .

Now, we beg to assure all whom it may concern, that we have no objection in the world to this. We think, on the contrary, that the object which these young gentlemen profess to have in view is a laudable one; and, were it not their manner of seeking it is objectionable, we should entertain sanguine [**624**] hopes that good might arise out of their exertions. But, besides that they are starting from a false point, inasmuch as they take no account whatever of the power of religion, or the influence of the clergy, as a connecting link between the high and the low in their respective neighbourhoods, the claim to originality of conception which they set up is quite inadmissible, particularly in reference to their great panacea for all the ills wherewith rural life is afflicted. We beg them to take our words for it, that they are not the first off-shoots of the aristocracy who have got up excellent matches at cricket with their poor neighbours. We would take the freedom also to remind them, that the land-allotment system of which they are advocates is no discovery of theirs. . . . And as to the laudation of parks, Athenaeums, and such like, how can even they, with all their hardihood, expect us to receive them as novelties? What was the object of the Whig commission for inquiring into the sanitary state of large towns, except to ascertain how far measures could be adopted for affording to the people of the manufacturing districts the conveniences which Young England is now advocating? and surely Sir Robert Peel's munificent subscription of a thousand pounds towards the formation of a *volks-garten* at Manchester is at least as much to the purpose as the most elaborate of Mr. Disraeli's essays, whether spoken at a *soirée* to a crowd of admiring operatives, or submitted to the consideration of the critics of a different class through the press.[18] We conceive, therefore, that we are doing no wrong to the cause which they profess to advocate, when we address ourselves to the subject pretty much as we should have done had no such candidates for popularity ever arisen.

We begin by avowing our profession of two points in political faith, namely – first, that society in this country is, and has long been, out of tune; and next, that a desire to remedy the evil, to bring harmony out of discord, by placing the various orders of the people in a better relation towards one another, is much more generally entertained than it used to be, even a quarter a century ago. There is good ground to believe, for example, that our master manufacturers, both in England and Scotland, are fast shaking themselves free from prejudices under which they once laboured.[19] They are beginning to understand that with the moral and religious improvement of their work-people their own success in trade is mixed up. They no longer look upon men, women, and children, as so many appendages to fixed machinery, but are learning to treat them as rational beings, whom it is their duty to care for and to control, not only while employed within the limits of their mills, but beyond them. Hence churches and schools are rising fast in all our great towns. . . . [**625**]

If we have ever been among the number of those . . . who held up the landed aristocracy of England as objects of imitation to the cotton lords, we are constrained on the present occasion to reverse the picture, and to recommend to the owners of the soil the adoption, as far as may be, of a course on which the owners of mills and manufactories seem fairly to have entered. Not that we charge the country gentlemen of England with indifference to the great duties which their position imposes upon them. We have already said, and we here repeat the statement, that every where, in the rural districts, not less than in the great towns, a general disposition has sprung up to place the relations of social life on a better footing, and to forget class-interests and class-prejudices in the great work of elevating the national character. To the working of this principle, indeed, much more than to a selfish dread of competition with the grower of foreign corn, we attribute that stir that is making to convey to the aid of English agriculture a greater amount than has heretofore attended it both of intelligence and dexterity.[20] But the misfortune is – and, perhaps at the outset the matter could not be other wise – that all this stir on the part of landlords and scientific men brings the former into more intimate connection only with their tenantry. The poor peasant derives no advantages, either physical or moral, from the improvements that are in progress. . . . He continues precisely what he was. More work is not found for him; better wages are not paid to him. Neither he nor his little ones are directed to improve their minds, nor taught to feel that they have a permanent stake in the country. As yet there is no hope for the peasant. He cannot rise beyond the sphere in which the accident of birth has cast him. No living soul appears to care for him, except at those annual gatherings, when, with as much [**627**] ostentatious show as kindness, he is paraded before a company of landowners, land-occupiers, and clergymen, to compete for some paltry prize. Contrast with this the behaviour of the mill-owners at Leeds and Manchester towards their work-people. See how considerately the latter are beginning to be treated. No middle-men stand between them and their employers, except so far as the necessities of business compel; and in all their more rational amusements the master-manufacturers join them. The consequence is continuous and steady elevation of character every where. For while the poor respect themselves the more because of the companionship to which the rich admit them, the rich acquire habits of thinking and acting, which, seeming to bring them down, raises them, in point of fact, higher and higher in the scale of rational beings. Nor let us omit to state that foot by foot with this wise attention to the temporal comforts of their people, goes the anxiety of very many of the leading manufacturers of England to promote among them a sound religious principle. The places of worship which have arisen and are daily arising in the great towns vouch for this, and from these, aided by the schools, for which properly trained teachers cannot be found enough, the happiest results are to be anticipated.

The landowners of England must bestir themselves. They, too, have a great part to play in the national revival which has begun; and if they do not enter upon it at once, and vigorously, their good name will suffer. They must strive to become personally acquainted with the labouring classes around them. It will no longer do to deal exclusively with the farmers; they must speak face to face with the men who dig, and plough, and reap, and thrash; and enable those same farmers to appear at rent-day with money in their purses. For the farmer has in too many instances abused his trust, and the landlord incurs the shame, and the peasant the sorrow.

. . . The peasantry, like the operatives must be educated in youth, and trained as they grow up to respect themselves and others; and to bring about this is just as much the duty of the owners of the soil, as it is incumbent on Mr Cobden, and such as he, to treat the [628] workers in their mills like rational and responsible beings. [629]

[L]et us entreat our agricultural friends to read with candour what is here written. We blame them not for having thus far adhered to a system which they received cut-and-dry from their fathers; neither are we about to withdraw from them, in regard to the corn-law question, the support which, from an honest conviction of the justice of their cause, we have hitherto afforded them. But we must not, because our general sympathies go with them, act unjustly towards others. There are points in which the most virulent of the League orators deserve to be looked at by them as models for imitation, and among these a growing desire to improve the condition of their work-people, both moral and social, is one. Let the 'Gentlemen of England' go and do so likewise; and they themselves, not less than the objects of their care, will find abundant reason to rejoice. [630]

(ii)   Retreating from the Present

[Anon.], Review of Coningsby[21]

. . . The New Generation . . . as far as it is represented by the author of 'Coningsby,' may fairly be charged with inconsistency. It professes to deplore the want of faith, and itself sets an example of universal scepticism. Mr. D'Israeli has no faith in men or measures, parties or institutions; not even faith in the Church as it is, but only in some spiritual ideal of the past, which to sober imaginations never existed. [98]

. . . The Church we know is a great principle with the 'new generation,' but what Church? Our new fashionable destructives in politics [99] are but New Jerusalemites in religion. The Church of England, as by law established, is not, in their eyes, that promised city in which dwelleth righteousness. The authorities of this school tell us of forms, fasts, festivals, saints, saintly observances, and many things unknown to the Church of England, or long since forgotten in the sleep of orthodoxy. The truth is, that the religious creed of 'Young England' is merely a poetical illusion. They worship a picture which time has improved by mellowing the tints, and softening or concealing every harsh feature. They look back into the dim past and are struck with the forms of the mighty dead. Their minds are impressed with the grandeur of the Church of Rome, when the world bowed to Spiritual influence. That influence they would restore for good purposes, utterly unconscious of the fact that the human mind must first be crushed to effect the object, and wholly blind to the mightier influences now at work, by which that object must be defeated. . . . [**100**]

[Anon.], 'Old Prejudices and New Crochets'[22]

Young England aims at reconciling the oldest prejudices and the newest crochets. For instance, we call it an old prejudice that monastic life, in itself, is meritorious. We call it a new crochet that monastic institutions are the appropriate remedy for the material and moral wants of the present age. . . . It appears to us that Lord John Manners, and all of that school of politicians are preoccupied to a puerile degree by the rage of attributing every *new* unfavourable symptom in our condition to neglect of some *old* practice. . . . Lord John Manners' scheme would seem to take it for granted that nothing has occurred since the middle ages to alter our condition for the worst, *except* the abolition of monastic charities . . . . Lord John Manners, and these monkery revivers, would seem to have awakened from a considerably longer nap than Rip Van Winkle's, and go about rubbing their eyes, and asking where are the convents they went to sleep in . . . . Will Lord John Manners tell us that the greatest portion of Europe and America is less enlightened, less humane, less *habitable* than three centuries back? Perhaps he will tell us so. We shall only beg him to do what he cannot have done yet – namely, *read history*. [**4**]

Notes to Part IV

1. *Ainsworth Magazine* 5 (June 1844), pp. 497–503. The reviewer refers to the *Tale of Alroy* (1833), a novel which predates Disraeli's association with Young England.
2. Ibid., 7 (June 1845), pp. 541–5.
3. *New Monthly Magazine* 71 (August 1844), pp. 527–34.
4. That is, the spirit of extreme Anglo-Catholicism, associated with the ideas of Edward Pusey (1800–82), a leading member of the Oxford Movement.
5. 'Literary Legislators Nos. I and II'.
6. This incomplete work dating from 1834 seemed to promise a reconciliation between the principles of the revolutionary and pre-revolutionary periods. Smythe's juxtaposition of figures from the ancient regime and from the 1790s in *Historic Fancies* may have reflected the influence of Disraeli's poem.
7. 'Literary Legislators No. III'.
8. *House of Commons Debates*, 69 c526, 18.5.43.
9. 'Literary Legislators No. IV'.
10. This essay reviews Manners' *England's Trust*, the second edition of Smythe's *Historic Fancies*, and Milnes' *Palm Leaves*, *Poems of Many Years*, and *Poems, Legendary and Historical*. The tone of the essay, and especially the defence of the effusive dedications to the first two of these works, suggests that Faber was the author.
11. This passage is preceded by the lines from *England's Trust* reproduced above, p. 109.
12. See above, pp. 29–30.
13. This charge was made in the *Edinburgh Review*.
14. 'Young England', *Edinburgh Review* 80 (February 1844), p. 518.
15. Croker 1883, III, 7–8. J. W. Croker (1780–1857) was a Conservative politician and man of letters. He is often taken to be the model for 'Mr. Rigby' in *Coningsby*, a character whose personality is 'tainted by an innate vulgarity' and is 'destitute of all imagination and noble sentiment.'(Disraeli 1844, Bk. I, ch. 1.) Disraeli later cast doubts on this attribution; see Swartz and Swartz 1975, p. 39.
16. See above.
17. *Fraser's Magazine* 30 (November 1844), pp. 924–30.
18. See above, pp. 133–7, for extracts from Young England's speeches at Manchester. Peel's gift to the city and to its neighbouring towns was recognized by the establishment of Peel Park in Salford; see Reed 1987, p. 111.

19. Cf. Ferrand's speech above, pp. 55–8.
20. A reference to what was known as 'high farming', that is, the application of improved agricultural techniques to maximize the return to farmers.
21. *Westminster Review* 42 (September 1844), pp. 80–105.
22. Originally from the *Globe*, reprinted in the *Morning Herald*, 5 August 1843, a Conservative newspaper that was consistently hostile to Young England and supportive of Peel. The title is the editor's.

Bibliography

The bibliography provides details of the sources of the texts printed in this volume, except those drawn from manuscripts and from the *House of Commons Debates*; these details are given in textual notes. It also lists the published works referred to in the Introduction and textual notes and other works by, or about, Young England. Unless otherwise indicated, the place of publication is London.

I *Young England Writings*

[Anon.] (1845a) 'The Policy of the New Generation', *The Oxford and Cambridge Review*, 1 (July), pp. 1–11
[Anon.] (1845b) 'Young England Philosophy, I–VII', *Morning Post*, 29, 31 July; 4, 15, 16, 25, 27 August
Cochrane, Alexander Baillie (1841a) *The Morea. To Which Is Added Meditations of Other Days*
Cochrane, Alexander Baillie (1841b) *Exeter Hall; or, Church Polemics*
Cochrane, Alexander Baillie (1849) *Lucille Belmont*, 3 vols
Disraeli, Benjamin (n.d.) *The Life of Lord George Bentinck*, Beaconsfield edn
Disraeli, Benjamin (1836) *The Letters of Runnymede*
Disraeli, Benjamin (1844) *Coningsby, or The New Generation*
Disraeli, Benjamin (1845) *Sybil, or The Two Nations*
Disraeli, Benjamin (1870) *Lothair*
Disraeli, Benjamin (1989) *Benjamin Disraeli: Letters,* vol. IV: *1842–1847*, eds J. B. Conacher and John Matthews (Toronto)
Ferrand, William Busfield (1841) *New Poor Law: The Speech of W. Busfield Ferrand, Esq. in the House of Commons, Tuesday, September 28th, 1841 . . .*
Lamington, Baron (1906) *In the Days of the Dandies*

Manners, Lord John (1840) 'A Trip Across the Spanish Frontier, I and II', *Fraser's Magazine* 21 and 22 (May and July), pp. 573–81, 102–12

Manners, Lord John (1841) *England's Trust and Other Poems*

Manners, Lord John (1843a) *The Monastic and Manufacturing Systems*

Manners, Lord John (1843b) *A Plea for National Holy-Days*

Manners, Lord John (1843c) *The Speech of Lord John Manners on The Laws of Mortmain in the House of Commons, on Tuesday, August 1st, 1843*

Manners, Lord John (1846) 'The Corn Laws and the Aristocracy, I and II', *The Oxford and Cambridge Review* (January and February), pp. 82–92, 191–7

Manners, Lord John (1850) *England's Ballads and Other Poems*

Manners, Lord John (1881) *Notes of an Irish Tour in 1846*, 2nd edn (Edinburgh)

Milnes, Richard Monckton (1840) *Poetry for the People, and Other Poems*

Milnes, Richard Monckton (1844a) *Memorials of Many Scenes*, new edn

Milnes, Richard Monckton (1844b) *Poems, Legendary and Historical*, new edn

Milnes, Richard Monckton (1845) *The Real Union of England and Ireland*

Smythe, George Sydney (1841) 'Speech to Canterbury Conservative Club, 8 January 1841', *Kentish Observer*, 14 January

Smythe, George Sydney (1843) Letter to the Electors of Canterbury 18 July 1843, *Morning Herald*, 20 July

Smythe, George Sydney (1844) *Historic Fancies*

Smythe, George Sydney (1845a) 'Earl Grey', *The Oxford and Cambridge Review* 1 (August), pp. 195–219

Smythe, George Sydney (1845b) 'The Jesuits', *The Oxford and Cambridge Review* 1 (September), pp. 225–48

Smythe, George Sydney (1845c) 'George Canning', *The Oxford and Cambridge Review* 1 (October), pp. 399–420

Smythe, George Sydney (1847) *Speech of the Honourable George Sydney Smythe, M.P. At Canterbury, on July 6, 1847*

Smythe, George Sydney (1852) 'Address Delivered to the Members of The Manchester Athenaeum, on 23 October 1844', in *The Importance of Literature to Men of Business: A Series of Addresses Delivered at Various Popular Insititutions*

Smythe, George Sydney (1875) *Angela Pisani: A Novel*, 3 vols

Young England (1845) *Young England, or, The Social Condition of the Empire* Nos. 1–14 (4 January–5 April)

Young England (1885) *Young England. Speeches Delivered by Lord John Manners M.P., at the Birmingham Athenic Institution, August 26th, 1844; . . . B. Disraeli . . . Lord John Manners and G. Sydney Smythe M.P., at the Manchester Athenaeum Soireé, October 3rd, 1844; Lord John Manners and B. Disraeli, at Bingley, Yorkshire, October 11th, 1844* [1845]

2 Other Primary Works

An Embryo MP (1844) *Anti-Coningsby; or, The New Generation Grown Old*, 2 vols

[Anon.] (1840) 'Ancient and Modern Ways of Charity', *The British Critic, and Quarterly Theological Review* 29 (January), pp. 44–70

[Anon.] (1842) 'The Rationale of Custom', *The Churchman. A Magazine in defence of the Church and Constitution* 7 (October), pp. 250–2

[Anon.] (1843) 'Young England', *The London Illustrated News* 3/68 (19 August), pp. 113–14

[Anon.] (1844) 'A Few Words Anent the Labouring Classes', *Fraser's Magazine* 30 (November), pp. 924–30

[Anon.] (1844) *Argumentum ad Populum: Tracts for Manhood No 1: On Seeming*

[Anon.] (1845c) *Argumentum ad Populum: Tracts for Manhood on Regeneration, Social, Moral and Spiritual*

[Anon.] (1846) *A Letter to Benjamin D'Israeli, Esq., M.P. Upon the Subject of his Recent Attack Upon the Minister. By a Barrister*

[Anon.] (1847) 'Literary Legislators, Nos. I–III, V', *Fraser's Magazine* 33 (January–April), pp. 79–95, 193–208, 321–46, 529–38

[Baring, E.] (1875) 'Mr Disraeli as a Man of the World', *Spectator* 501 (May), pp. 554–5

Beiser, Frederick C. (1996) ed. and trans., *The Early Political Writings of the German Romantics* (Cambridge)

[Berkeley, George] (1725) *The Querist, Containing Several Queries, Proposed to the Consideration of the Public By the Bishop of Cloyne* (Dublin)

Boswell, James (1979) *Life of Johnson* (Harmondsworth)

Carlyle, Thomas (1839) *Chartism*

Carlyle, Thomas (1843) *Past and Present*

[Croker, J. W.] (1843) 'The Policy of Ministers', *Quarterly Review* 144, pp. 553–93

Davis, Thomas (1846) *Literary and Historical Essays* (Dublin)

Digby, Kenelm Henry (1877) *The Broad Stone of Honour: or, The True Sense and Practice of Chivalry*, 5 vols

Faber, Frederick (1840) *The Cherwell Water-Lily, and Other Poems*

Faber, Frederick (1842) *The Styrian Lake, and Other Poems*

Gresley, William (1841) *Remarks on the Necessity of Attempting a Restoration of the National Church*

Hallam, Henry (1827) *Constitutional History*, 2 vols

Hanmer, Sir John (1840) *Sonnets by Sir John Hanmer, Bart.*

James the First (1633) *The King's Maiesties Declaration to His Subjects Concerning Lawfull Sports to bee used*

[Mennel, Philip] (1872) *Lord John Manners: A Political and Literary Sketch, Comprising Some Account of The Young England Party and The Passing of the Factory Acts*

Newman, John Henry (1836) *Lyra Apostolica*

O'Brien, William Smith (1843) *Speech . . . on the Causes of Discontent in Ireland, Delivered in the House of Commons, on the 4th. July 1843* (Dublin)

Paget, Francis Edward (1841) *Tales of the Village*, 2nd series

Paget, Francis Edward (1843) *The Warden of Berkinholt*

Palmer, William (1841) *An Enquiry into The Possibility of Obtaining Means for Church Extension without Parliamentary Grants*

Peel, Sir Robert (1846) . . . *Speech in the House of Commons, on . . . January 27th, 1846*

Prentice, Archibald (1853) *History of the Anti-Corn-Law League*, 2 vols

Pugin, A. W. (1836) *Contrasts; or, A Parallel Between the Noble Edifices of the Fourteenth and Fifteenth Centuries, and Similar Buildings of the Present Day; shewing The Present Decay of Taste*

Sewell, William (1841) 'Principles of Gothic Architecture', *Quarterly Review*, 69 (December), pp. 111–49

Sewell, William (1845) *Hawkstone; a tale of and for England in 184—*

Southey, Robert (1824) *The Book of the Church*, 2 vols

Southey, Robert (1829) *Sir Thomas More; or, Colloquies on The Progress and Prospects of Society*, 2 vols

S[tewart], E. M. (1845) *Rodenhurst; or, The Church and the Manor*, 3 vols

Strutt, Joseph (1801) *Glig-Gamena Angel-Deod.; or, The Sports and Pastimes of the People of England*

[Wordsworth, Christopher] (1845) *Church Principles and Church Measures: A Letter To Lord John Manners, M.P.*

3   Lives and Letters, Contemporary Memoirs

Croker, John Wilson (1883) *The Croker Papers: The Correspondence and Diaries of . . . John Croker*, ed. Louis J. Jennings, 3 vols

Duffy, Charles Gavan (1880) *Young Ireland: A Fragment of Irish History, 1840–1850*

Duffy, Charles Gavan (1890) *Thomas Davis: The Memoirs of an Irish Patriot 1840–1846*

Fonblanque, Edward Barrington de (1878) *Lives of the Lords Strangford, with Their Ancestors and Contemporaries Through Ten Generations*

Greville, Charles (1885) *The Greville Memoirs*, Second Part: *A Journal of the Reign of Queen Victoria from 1837 to 1852*, 3 vols

Holland, Bernard (1919) *Memoir of Kenelm Henry Digby*

Purcell, Edmund Sheridan (1900) *The Life and Letters of Ambrose Phillip de Lisle*, ed. Edwin de Lisle, 2 vols

Reid, Wemyss, T. (1890) *The Life, Letters, and Friendships of Richard Monckton Milnes, First Lord Houghton*, 2 vols

Strangford, Lady (1875) 'A Brief Memoir of George Sydney Smythe', in George Smythe, *Angela Pisani*, vol. I

Swartz, Helen, and Swartz, Marvin (1979) *Disraeli's Reminiscences* (New York)

Whibley, Charles (1925) *Lord John Manners and His Friends*, 2 vols (Edinburgh)

4   Contemporary Reviews

'*Coningsby*', *New Monthly Magazine* 71 (June 1844)
'*Coningsby*', *Fraser's Magazine* 30 (July 1844), pp. 71–84
'*Coningsby*', *Tait's Edinburgh Magazine* (July 1844), pp. 447–61
'*Coningsby*', *Westminister Review* 42 (September 1844), pp. 80–105
'D'Israeli and the New Generation', *Ainsworth Magazine* 5 (June 1844)
    pp. 497–503
'*Historic Fancies*', *New Monthly Magazine* 71 (August 1844), pp. 527–34
'*Historic Fancies*', *Fraser's Magazine* 30 (September 1844), pp. 310–21
'*England's Trust*', *The British Critic and Quarterly Theological Review* 30 (October
    1841), pp. 466–94
'Literary Legislators, Nos. I–IV', *Fraser's Magazine*, 35 (January–May 1847),
    pp. 79–95, 193–208, 321–339, 529–538
'National Holydays', *Dublin Review* 14 (May 1843), pp. 481–505
'*Sybil*', *Ainsworth Magazine* 7 (June 1845), pp. 541–5
'*Sybil*', *British Quarterly Review* 2 (August 1845), pp. 159–73
'*Sybil*', *Westminister Review* 44 (September 1845), pp. 141–52
'The Prospects of Poetry', *The Oxford and Cambridge Review* 1 (July 1845),
    pp. 45–67
'Young England', *Edinburgh Review* 80 (February 1844), pp. 517–25
'Young England', *New Monthly Magazine* 70 (February 1844), pp. 174–81

5   Secondary Works

Best, G. F. A. (1964) *Temporal Pillars: Queen Anne's Bounty, the Ecclesiastical
    Commissioners and the Church of England* (Cambridge)
Blake, Robert (1965) *Disraeli*
Chadwick, Owen (1966) *The Victorian Church*
Chadwick, Owen (1990) 'The Mind of the Oxford Movement' (1960), in *The Spirit
    of the Oxford Movement: Tractarian Essays* (Cambridge)
Chandler, Alice (1970) *A Dream of Order: The Medieval Ideal in Nineteenth-
    Century English Literature* (Lincoln, Nebr.)
Childers, Joseph W. (1995) *Novel Possibilities: Fiction and the Formation of Early
    Victorian Culture* (Philadelphia)
Clausson, Nils (1986) 'Disraeli and Carlyle's "Aristocracy of Talent": The Role of
    Millbank in *Coningsby* Reconsidered', *Victorian Newsletter* 70, pp. 1–4
Davis, Richard (1987) *The Young Ireland Movement* (Dublin)
Driver, Cecil (1946) *Tory Radical: The life of Richard Oastler* (New York)
Ehrman, John (1969) *The Younger Pitt*, vol. I: *The Years of Acclaim*

Ehrman, John (1983) *The Younger Pitt*, vol. II: *The Reluctant Transition*

Faber, Richard (1987) *Young England*

Francis, Mark, and Morrow, John (1994) *A History of English Political Thought in the Nineteenth Century*

Gray, Peter Henry (1992) *British Politics and the Irish Land Question, 1843–1850*, Ph.D. dissertation, University of Cambridge

Gray, Peter Henry (1999) *Famine, land and politics: British Government and Irish Society, 1843–1850*, (Dublin)

Girouard, Mark (1981) *The Return to Camelot: Chivalry and the English Gentleman* (New Haven, Conn.)

Hilton, Boyd (1988) *The Age of Atonement: The Influence of Evangelicalism on Social and Economic Thought 1795–1865* (Oxford)

Jenkins, T. A. (1996) *Disraeli and Victorian Conservatism*

Kegel, Charles H. (1961) 'Lord John Manners and the Young England Movement: Romanticism in Politics', *Western Political Quarterly* 14, pp. 691–7

Kerr, Donal A. (1982) *Peel, Priests and Politics* (Oxford)

Mandler, Peter (1990) *Aristocratic Government in the Age of Reform: Whigs and Liberals 1830–1852* (Oxford)

Millar, Mary S., and Wiebe, M. G. (1992) 'The Power So Vast: Disraeli and the Press in the 1840s', *Victorian Periodicals Review* 25/2 (Summer), pp. 79–85

Morris, Kevin L. (1984) *The Images of the Middle Ages in Romantic and Victorian Literature*

Prentice, Archibald (1968) *History of the Anti-Corn-Law League* (1853), ed. W. H. Chaloner

Pocock, J. G. A. (1974) *The Machiavellian Moment* (Princeton, N.J.)

Reed, Donald (1987) *Peel and the Victorians* (Oxford)

Ridley, Jane (1995) *The Young Disraeli*

Rose, Michael E. (1985) 'Culture, Philanthropy and the Manchester Middle Classes', in Alan J. Kidd and K. W. Roberts (eds), *City, Class and Culture* (Manchester), pp. 103–19

Smith, Peter (1996) *Disraeli: A Brief Life* (Cambridge)

Soloway, Richard Allen (1969) *Prelates and People: Ecclesiastical Social Thought in England 1783–1852*

Tucker, Albert (1962) 'Disraeli and the Natural Aristocracy', *Canadian Journal of Economic and Political Science* 28, pp. 1–9

Ward, J. T. (1965–6) '"Young England" at Bingley', *Journal of the Bradford Textile Society*, pp. 49–59

Ward, J. T. (1966) 'Young England', *History Today* 16/2 (February), pp. 120–7

Index